HOW

······ TO ······

READ

······ A ······

WORD

HOW

······· TO ·······

READ

······· A ·······

WORD

Elizabeth Knowles

OXFORD
UNIVERSITY PRESS

OXFORD
UNIVERSITY PRESS

Great Clarendon Street, Oxford OX2 6DP

Oxford University Press is a department of the University of Oxford.
It furthers the University's objective of excellence in research, scholarship,
and education by publishing worldwide in

Oxford New York

Auckland Cape Town Dar es Salaam Hong Kong Karachi
Kuala Lumpur Madrid Melbourne Mexico City Nairobi
New Delhi Shanghai Taipei Toronto

With offices in

Argentina Austria Brazil Chile Czech Republic France Greece
Guatemala Hungary Italy Japan Poland Portugal Singapore
South Korea Switzerland Thailand Turkey Ukraine Vietnam

Oxford is a registered trade mark of Oxford University Press
in the UK and in certain other countries

Published in the United States
by Oxford University Press Inc., New York

British Library Cataloguing in Publication Data
Data available

Library of Congress Cataloging in Publication Data
Typeset by Glyph International, Bangalore, India
Printed in Great Britain
on acid-free paper by
Clays Ltd, St Ives plc

ISBN 978-0-19-957489-6

10 9 8 7 6 5 4 3 2 1

To Patrick Orpen Dudgeon,
with great affection

Acknowledgements

Acknowledgements

In writing this book I have naturally drawn on the expertise and scholarship of many fellow lexicographers, especially former colleagues at Oxford University Press.

Particular thanks are due to those who have been my valued consultants: Ben Harris (who also had the original idea for the book), Orin Hargraves, and Penny Silva. They have all patiently read drafts and responded with helpful and perceptive comments, and I am extremely grateful. Yvonne Warburton, my original mentor in library research, and a most valued friend, fruitfully discussed sections of the book, and as a particularly gifted researcher revisited the experience of word exploration in a pre-digital age. Margot Charlton kindly shared her experiences of responding to questions about language from the general public. Ernie and Emily Gascoigne's question about 'satsuma' started me down what turned out to be a satisfying path. I am also very grateful to Joan Houston Hall, Chief Editor of the *Dictionary of American Regional English*, for allowing us to use a panel from their fascinating website as an illustration.

My editors at OUP, Vicki Donald and Rebecca Lane, have been supportive and encouraging: I am more than grateful for all that they have done. Needless to say, any errors or omissions are my own.

It has been enormously enjoyable to work on this book: I hope I have been able to share some of these pleasures with my readers.

Elizabeth Knowles
Oxford, April 2010

Contents

CONTENTS

• •

Introduction

We encounter words constantly, through ordinary conversation, reading, overheard speech, broadcasting, the internet. In the same day, a person with an interest in language may hear the latest buzzword, or encounter a nineteenth-century usage through a dramatization or reworking of Jane Austen. Questions presenting themselves are not necessarily of literary origin: they may be triggered by consideration of the fruit section of a supermarket, reading a report in a newspaper, or by a report from another English-speaking country.

Encountering an unfamiliar word or phrase, or noticing for the first time some aspect of a known word, is a provocation to find out more. A single sentence can contain enough material to trigger a whole range of questions. For example, in October 2008, Paul McKeever, Chairman of the British Police Federation, was reported as saying:

> We are realists, we are pragmatists. We are not quixotic idealists who are looking for pyrrhic victories to prove a point.

The sentence generates a number of possible questions. *Realist* and *pragmatist* are used as virtual synonyms. What in fact are their precise shades of meaning, and when did the words enter the language? Or, the attention might be caught by *quixotic*, an adjective deriving from the name of a fictional character, Cervantes' Don Quixote. What other words go back to the name of a fictional character, or has Don Quixote any other influence on our language? (The expression *tilting at windmills* may come to mind.) Finally, there is the use of *pyrrhic victory*, an expression coming from the classical world. (Investigation of current usage of the term might well turn up the spirited debate, conducted on www.sportsjournalist.com in January 2008, on how widely understood the phrase would be today.)

There is no limit to the questions we may ask about a word or phrase. (The furore surrounding the announcement, in June 2009, by the Global Language Monitor company that they would shortly identify the millionth word to enter the English language included not only heated debate as to the number of words currently estimated to be in the language already, but also, after the announcement of *Web 2.0* as the key item, considerable disagreement as to what can be held to constitute a word.)

Most simply, we might want to know what a word means, or where it comes from. We might wonder what other meanings it has had in the past, or whether it appears to be developing a further sense. How is it pronounced, and is there more than one way of saying it? Has it been used famously by a well-known person, or does it have particular social, cultural, or historical asssociations? Does it originate in a particular local dialect, or a form of World English?

Beyond this, we might consider whether the word belongs to a set which we choose to delineate. Is it, for example, one of a number of names for a particular type of thing? Does it belong with other words borrowed from a particular language? What other words were first recorded in the same century (or decade, or year) as the word in which we are interested? Each discrete piece of information can constitute a starting point. Are there more words like this? Perhaps with similar meanings, or origins, or dating from the same period? Did the word exist in Shakespeare's day, or Jane Austen's, and if so, did it mean the same as it does now?

We may also be interested in associations which go beyond the strictly lexical. Does the word form a key part of a well-known speech or passage of literature, or is it associated in the public mind with a particular event, or period of time? Was it used particularly of or by a notable fictional character? Any aspect of a word may start us on a journey of exploration, and from multi-volume print dictionaries to the personally created websites of other language buffs, via such resources as the digitized texts searchable through Google Books, there have never been such rich resources to explore.

I have been professionally engaged with words, and dictionaries, since I first became a library researcher for the *Supplement to the Oxford English Dictionary*, over thirty years ago. I have never forgotten the sense of excitement generated by a successful search for a word or phrase, and the fascination of the colourful stories that were revealed. It is the intention of this book to share some of that pleasure, by setting out in detail the ways in which we can all interrogate words. Using real-language examples, I have looked both at the questions we can ask, and at where and how we can look for the answers.

There has probably never been a time when someone who wishes to explore words has had richer resources to hand. I hope that *How to Read a Word* will offer its readers a chance to make full use of what is now available to us all.

Elizabeth Knowles

Chapter 11

But is it in the Dictionary?

Chapter 1
But is it in the Dictionary?

WHEN we encounter an unfamiliar (not to say improbable) word we may well ask, 'Is it in the dictionary?'—a standard way of asking whether the item in question has an acknowledged existence. We think of a language as made up of recognized vocabulary (the 'lexicon').

At a press briefing on 29 September 2009, a reporter's question to the White House Press Secretary Robert Gibbs was interrupted as her colleagues began to laugh. She had begun, 'From the standpoint of leverage or strategery, how do you—', and was cut off by the Press Secretary's comment that he loved the way 'a "Saturday Night Live" word' had 'entered into the lexicon'.

Strategery first caught the public attention in 2000, during the American presidential election between the then Vice-President, Al Gore, and his Republican opponent, George W. Bush. Bush's tendency to mangle words had already been noted by satirists, and in October provided the concluding moment (and punchline) of a supposed debate between Bush and Gore shown on a *Saturday Night Live* sketch. The debate moderator asked each of the candidates to 'sum up in a single word the best argument for his candidacy'. The comedian Will Ferrell, playing George W. Bush, responded with a satisfied nod, 'Strategery'.

Strategery was to embed itself successfully in the public mind as a characteristic 'Bushism'. In the following spring, a satirical sitcom, *That's My Bush*, was produced by Comedy Central (creators of *South Park*). The sitcom was staged in the White House of the new President and First Lady, and the American actor Timothy Bottoms was cast as George W. Bush. In March, the *New York Times* columnist John Leland published a column in the form of an interview with Timothy Bottoms. This included the following exchange:

> Q: What does the word strategery mean to you?
> A: I've never heard of that word. Is it in the dictionary?
> —in *New York Times* 25 March 2001

The question assumed that readers would connect Bush with *strategery*; the response used a familiar phrase, 'Is it in the dictionary?' to underline his supposed lack of grasp on language.

In the eight years between 2001 and 2009, *strategery* took on a certain life of its own. It was used jokingly in Bush's own White House. As the *Washington Post* of 17 October 2004 reported, his Chief of Staff Karl Rove's Office of Strategic Initiatives was informally 'known around the West Wing as "Strategery"'.

In August 2008, the *Jerusalem Post* published a review of *What Happened: Inside Bush's White House and Washington's Culture of Deception* by the former White House Press Secretary, Scott McClellan. Discussing McClellan's position, the columnist wrote:

> He was excluded from discussions at the National Security Council, the daily 'communications' conversations

> and the small, informal 'strategery' sessions where the
> real give-and-take occurred.
> —in *Jerusalem Post* 7 August 2008

By 2009, as we have seen, it was possible for *strategery* to appear in a question to the White House Press Secretary without any apparent intentional satire, although its reception indicated a general awareness of its history. However, it did demonstrate that to a certain degree it had 'joined the lexicon', even if it has not yet achieved full dictionary status.[1]

Over fifty years before, 'Is it in the dictionary?' had appeared in a column in the *Los Angeles Times* of 26 June 1948, Fred Colby's syndicated 'Take My Word for It'. In a previous column, Colby had introduced a paragraph on the word *khaki* with the words 'Overheard on a news commentation'. The 'Four Hour Speech Class' from the Central Junior High School of Kansas City, given the article to discuss, had written in to ask whether there were really such a word as 'commentation'. The nub of their question was, 'Did you make it up, or is it in the dictionary?'

Colby, assuring the class of the word's existence, went into some detail. *Commentation* was in *Webster's New International*, *Funk and Wagnall's New Standard*, and the *New Century Dictionary*, but not in a number of others, for example the *American College Dictionary* or *Funk and Wagnall's New College Standard*.[2] By giving these details, he was in fact giving some clues as to the word's lack of currency: *commentation* was to be found only in the older and larger American dictionaries. However, the Four Hour Speech Class were presumably satisfied: what they had wanted to know was whether a word they had never met had qualified for any level of recognition.

strategy

While enjoying the emergence of *strategery*, it is worth taking time to look up the background of the parent word, *strategy*. It came into English (via French) from Greek *stratēgos* 'army general', and turns out to be one of those words which have two existences. It is briefly recorded in the late seventeenth century (with reference to the Roman statesman and scholar Pliny the Elder), to mean a government or province ruled by a general. It was reintroduced in the early nineteenth century to denote the art of planning and directing overall military operations and movements in war: something that was seen as the special role of a commander-in-chief.

Later developments such as the compound *strategic thinking* testify to the positive light in which *strategy* is seen, and it is interesting to compare it with the linked word *stratagem*. Introduced in the late fifteenth century in the sense of 'a military ploy', it is most likely to be used today in the sense of a scheme to outwit an opponent or achieve an end, with an implication of deviousness or cunning. As Elizabeth Bennet in Jane Austen's *Pride and Prejudice* (1813), contemplating how her sister Lydia's marriage has been achieved, warns her aunt, 'If you do not tell me in an honourable manner, I shall certainly be reduced to tricks and stratagems to find it out.' And yet both *strategy* and *stratagem* come from the same root.

The ultimate authority?

'Is it in the dictionary?' is a formulation suggesting that there is a single lexical authority: '*The* Dictionary'. As the British academic Rosamund Moon has commented, 'The dictionary

most cited in such cases is the UAD: the Unidentified Authoriz-
ing Dictionary, usually referred to as "the dictionary", but very
occasionally as "my dictionary".[3] The American scholar John
Algeo has coined the term *lexicographicolatry* for a reverence
for dictionary authority amounting to idolatry. As he
explained:

> English speakers have adopted two great icons of culture:
> the Bible and the dictionary. As the Bible is the sacred
> Book, so the dictionary has become the secular Book, the
> source of authority, the model of behavior, and the sym-
> bol of unity in language.
> —John Algeo 'Dictionaries as seen by the Educated Pub-
> lic in Great Britain and the USA' in F. J. Hausmann et al.
> (eds) *An International Encyclopedia of Lexicography* (1989)
> vol. 1, p. 29

While recognizing the respect for lexical authority illumi-
nated by this passage, it is not difficult to find less unquestion-
ing perspectives. The notion of any dictionary representing a
type of scriptural authority runs counter, for instance, to the
view of the 'Great Lexicographer' Samuel Johnson that:

> Dictionaries are like watches, the worst is better than
> none, and the best cannot be expected to go quite true.
> —Samuel Johnson, letter to Francesco Sastres, 21 August
> 1784

A dictionary may also be highly derivative: twenty years
before Johnson's letter, the French writer and critic Voltaire
had warned cynically in his *Philosophical Dictionary* that 'All
dictionaries are made from dictionaries.'[4] However, there is
evidence that Johnson's contemporary Lord Chesterfield had

also embraced the concept of universal lexical authorization. He wrote to his son in 1754:

> Attend minutely to your style, whatever language you speak or write in; seek for the best words, and think of the best turns. Whenever you doubt of the propriety or elegancy of any word, search the dictionary, or some good author for it, or inquire of somebody, who is master of that language.
> —Lord Chesterfield, letter, 12 February 1754

Overall, it is reasonable to conclude that there is a natural tendency to regard the dictionary with which we are most familiar as having particular authority.

Which dictionary?

References to 'the dictionary' assume not just that there is only one dictionary worth considering, but that (apart from quality) there will be no significant distinction between individual members of the class of dictionaries. Any dictionary will offer the same range of information. However, while it is true that any dictionary is likely to offer basic information as to pronunciation, part of speech, meaning, and probably origin, individual dictionaries differ widely in range and purpose.

When considering a dictionary of the English language, the first thing to establish is whether it is a historical dictionary, the primary purpose of which is to provide a record of the language across the centuries, or a dictionary of the current language, which will map the language as spoken today.[5]

budget /ˈbʌdʒɪt/ *noun & adjective*. See also **BOUGET. LME**.
[ORIGIN Old French *bougette* dim. of *bouge* leather bag from Latin *bulga*: see **BULGE, -ET¹**.]

▶ **A** *noun*. **1** A pouch or wallet. *obsolete* exc. *dial.* **LME**.
▸†**b** *spec*. A leather container, *esp*. a leather or skin bottle. **L16–M19**.
open one's budget speak one's mind.
2 The contents of a bag or wallet; a bundle, a collection, a stock. *arch*. **L16**. ▸**b** *spec*. A long letter full of news. **E19**.

> SWIFT I read .. the whole budget of papers you sent. *fig.*: HAZLITT His budget of general knowledge. **b** DAY LEWIS I had a budget from her last week.

3 A periodic (esp. annual) estimate of the revenue and expenditure of a country or organization; an account or statement of this, *esp*. one made by the Chancellor of the Exchequer in the House of Commons; a similar estimate for a private individual or family. Also, the amount of money needed or available for spending. **M18**.

> J. K. GALBRAITH The balanced budget .. has been the *sine qua non* of sound and sensible management of the public purse.
> B. CASTLE The Chancellor must be free to have a later budget next year. P. DAVIES Most 'pure' scientists work in large laboratory teams .. and annual budgets run into hundreds of millions of dollars.

on a budget with a restricted amount of money.
– COMB.: **budget buster** (chiefly *US*) a person, policy, or measure proposing or effecting expenditure in excess of an agreed budget.
▶ **B** *attrib*. or as *adjective*. Designed or suitable for someone of limited means; cheap. **M20**.

> *Woman's Own* Budget meals for the family.

budget account: see **ACCOUNT** *noun*.
■ **budgetary** *adjective* of or pertaining to a budget **L19**.
budge'teer *noun* a person who makes up or supports a budget **M19**.

Shorter Oxford English Dictionary entry for *budget*, showing sense-ordering according to chronology.

The question we have in mind ('What did the word mean in Jane Austen's time?' 'What does it mean today?') will determine which is the best resource for our purposes.[6]

budget ▶ noun **1** an estimate of income and expenditure for a set period of time: *keep within the household budget.*
■ (**Budget**) an annual or other regular estimate of national revenue and expenditure put forward by a finance minister. ■ the amount of money needed or available for a purpose: *they have a limited budget.*
2 archaic a quantity of written or printed material.
▶ verb (**budgets, budgeting, budgeted**) [no obj.] allow or provide for in a budget: *the university is budgeting for a deficit* | [as adj. **budgeted**] *a budgeted figure of £31,000.*
■ [with obj.] provide (a sum of money) for a particular purpose from a budget: *the council proposes to budget £100,000 to provide grants.*
▶ **adjective** [attrib.] inexpensive: *a budget guitar.*
– PHRASES **on a budget** with a restricted amount of money: *we're travelling on a budget.*
– DERIVATIVES **budgetary** adjective.
– ORIGIN late Middle English: from Old French *bougette*, diminutive of *bouge* 'leather bag', from Latin *bulga* 'leather bag, knapsack', of Gaulish origin. Compare with **BULGE**. The word originally meant a pouch or wallet, and later its contents. In the mid 18th cent., the Chancellor of the Exchequer, in presenting his annual statement, was said 'to open the budget'. In the late 19th cent. the use of the term was extended from governmental to other finances.

Oxford Dictionary of English entry for *budget*, showing sense-ordering according to contemporary currency.

Beyond this, we need to be aware of the degree to which considerations of space may have limited the degree of information to be given. We should also clarify how strictly the dictionary we are using holds to the principle that a dictionary exists to provide information about words and usage; does it perhaps offer wider coverage, and include encylopedic information?

dictionary

It is possible that *dictionary* will be one of the least-consulted entries in such a reference book, since if you are already using a dictionary, you may well not feel any need to explore its name. However, doing so does add interest and context to what has been a staple of our bookshelves for over five hundred years.

The first recorded use of the word in English comes from the first half of the sixteenth century, and its first appearance in a title is from a Latin-English dictionary of 1538, *The Dictionary of syr Thomas Eliot knyght*. In 1547, a Welsh-English dictionary advertised itself as 'moche necessary to all such Welshemen as will spedly lerne the Englyshe tongue'. By the early seventeenth century, a character in John Webster's *The Duchess of Malfi* could respond to an unknown word, 'What's that? I need a dictionary to't.'

The term came into the language from medieval Latin, originally in the fuller form *dictionarium manuale* 'manual of words' or *dictionarium liber* 'book of words'. *Dictionarium* comes ultimately from Latin *dicere* 'to say', which is also the basis of our English word *diction*.

(For an overview of the history of dictionaries of the English language, see Appendix, p. 153.)

Through the ages

If we are investigating a word from the past, which might have had a different meaning in the nineteenth or twentieth century from the meaning it has today, a dictionary of the historical language is likely to be the most useful for us. In June 2009, coverage of the story of MPs' expenses featured the word *redact*, in relation to publication of 'full' expenses claims with numerous details blacked out or 'redacted'. It is worth pausing here to look in a little more detail at *redact*, and what it can show us of the kind of information that a dictionary can give us, and at what points we can try to flesh out the information given.

Investigation would have revealed quite quickly that *redact* was an established word, deriving from the Latin root *redact-* of the verb *redigere* 'to bring back'. It was originally recorded in the English language in the late fifteenth century, in the sense of 'bring together into a single entity', applied especially to the organization of ideas or writings into a coherent whole.

Redact had died out of use by the middle of the eighteenth century, but was reintroduced in the specific sense of editing text for publication in the early nineteenth century. The *Oxford English Dictionary* provides usage evidence for words and senses, and the first illustration for this sense of *redact* comes from the *Monthly Review* of autumn 1829, 'The account of his second expedition was carefully redacted', and at this point it is worth seeing whether we can flesh out the context for a little more background. The full text of the *Monthly Review* is available online, and it is not difficult to find the relevant passage:

> Mungo Park, the ill-fated African traveller, wrote himself the account of his first expedition, and his narrative was universally read with interest; the account of his second expedition was carefully redacted, and of course set forth in what was supposed to be the best guise of polished paragraphs and rounded periods. The booksellers, however, found, to their cost, that the money thus spent for

> the purpose of improving the work, in effect injured it, as
> seldom fails to be the case.
> —in *Monthly Review* October 1829

Clearly in this case the process of 'redaction', while well intended, was seen as having been ultimately damaging.

Redact in today's language has been used neutrally in the sense of editing text for publication. However, at least in Britain, events of 2009 are likely to have given 'redact' an association of editing especially for the purpose of suppressing or removing potentially embarrassing material. A *Times* leader from June 2009 went a step further by extending the use of the term from a text to a person. The topic under discussion was the resignation under pressure of the Speaker to the House of Commons, Michael Martin, who had been strongly criticized for his handling of the expenses affair:

> More recently holders of the office have quietly retired.
> But yesterday Michael Martin made history. He became
> the first Speaker to be redacted.
> —in *Times* 22 June 2009

Consultation of a dictionary, therefore, while providing the essential facts about a word, can be usefully supplemented by alertness to events which are likely to colour association and perhaps influence further shifts in use and meaning. In the case of *redact*, watching out for similar uses, or searching online after coverage of the immediate news story had died down, could suggest whether the *Times* usage was a single instance of wordplay[7], or whether it heralded a genuine extension of the way in which the word was likely to be used in future.

Taking the temperature

Dictionaries include new senses, and new words, when the lexicographers feel that they have sufficient evidence to justify coverage: reasonably widespread use over a sufficient period of time. However, there are ways in which we can ourselves try to assess how widely known and used a word is, or is becoming, once we have registered it as a matter of interest.

One way, of course, is to search for further examples: online resources today make that entirely possible, although we may find (in the case of a possible new sense) that we are over-whelmed with hits from more traditional usage (*redact* would probably be an example of this). One way would be to look for resources where some filtering has already taken place: for example, Michael Quinion's website *World Wide Words* (www.worldwidewords.org), which highlights both new words and older terms which have come to notice. Another approach would be to take advantage of annual round-ups of new words and senses. In late December and early January, dictionary publishers and bodies concerned with language (such as the American Dialect Society) put out lists of what their evidence indicates are 'words of the year': words (or phrases) which have had the highest profile. These may be words which have developed a new sense (*twitter* would be a good example of this), or completely new words. In either case, what we can see is a level of recognition achieved before a word or sense has graduated to being 'in the dictionary'.

New words

Some words which come to public attention appear to be genuinely new—for example, the term *staycation*, which surfaced in 2008 and 2009 amid a flurry of publicity. There were immediate clues in the news stories that the word might well be too new, or previously too little used, to have been included yet in dictionaries. Headlines often presented the word in inverted commas, as 'Hard-up Britain: holidays turn into "staycations"' (*Times*, 12 July 2008), and 'Vacations with kids: the "stay-cation"' (*Christian Science Monitor*, 5 May 2008). Even more relevantly, a news story of July 2009 reported the inclusion of the term in the latest edition of *Merriam-Webster's Collegiate Dictionary*.

When a word like *staycation* catches the public interest, it is likely that coverage will include discussions about possible origins. Suggestions found in news stories include the possibility that 'a sports columnist at *The Myrtle Beach Sun-News* may have coined the term in July 2003, describing his nine-day stay at home to watch sports' (*Lynchburg News and Advance*, online edition, 19 May 2009), and the information that its 'origin is often attributed to a popular Canadian television series' (www.msnbc.msn.com, 12 March 2008). While popular attributions often turn out to be unfounded, they may offer possibilities for investigation, and in any case, it is of interest to know what is generally believed about a word or phrase. More solid assessments, or detailed discussion, may be found on online websites with good coverage of neologisms and burgeoning vocabulary, such as *World Wide Words* (www.worldwidewords.org) referred to above, or Paul McFedries's

Word Spy (http://www.wordspy.com), which describes itself as 'The word lover's guide to new words'.[8]

More than one dictionary

A dictionary of the language, current or historical, is where we go for the essential information about words: pronunciation, spelling, origin, date, and meaning. However, we may well encounter a word which emerges from a particular type of regional or World English—something which is made even more likely by the dissemination of news around the World Wide Web. A good example of this occurred in November 2009, when a number of news stories appeared relating to the launch of a version of the Scottish Parliament website in the Scots language.

The first page is headed, 'Walcome tae the Scottish Pairlament wabsite', and there are further links to key pages. Many of the words, such as 'wabsite' and 'pairlament', are clear enough even if you are not familiar with Scots, but it is easy to find other vocabulary items which evidently represent preferred alternatives to 'standard' English. Headings and sentences such as

> *We want to mak siccar*
> *Garrin the Scottish Pairlament wark for you*
> *Whit can I speir?*
> *Gin ye are needin an interpreter*

present us with words such as *siccar*, *garrin*, *speir*, and *gin*, but to explore them properly we need a dictionary of the Scots language.[9] Happily, there is an excellent one available, to be found in the online *Dictionary of the Scots Language* (*DSL*) (www.dsl.ac.uk).[10] Recourse to this resource allows us to translate the words we have identified:

siccar	sure
gar	make
speir	ask
gin	if

Researching the first of these, *siccar* (a variant of *sicker* 'sure'), shows how a casual query can lead to a colourful piece of language history. The *DSL*, noting that *siccar* occurs most frequently in the phrase *to mak siccar*, 'to make sure or certain', adds that it is often used in allusion to a particular historical event. In 1306 Robert the Bruce, later King of Scotland, and his followers, clashed with Bruce's rival, the 'Red Comyn'. Bruce himself had quarrelled with and wounded his opponent, and his follower Sir John Kirkpatrick then killed Comyn with the words 'I'll mak sicker' (the words were subsequently adopted as a motto by the Kirkpatrick family).

Siccar, like *gar*, *speir*, and *gin*, is definitely a term which is 'in the dictionary', although probably not in a dictionary of current or even historical English.

There are many other kinds of language dictionary, covering areas from slang to rhyme, and there is another category of reference book which is an essential component to exploring the language. A thesaurus offers us lists of words grouped according to meaning: an invaluable tool if we want to know what other ways there may be of saying the same thing. And, as with a dictionary, the range of related terms provided may cover both past and present. A thesaurus of current English is likely to offer words in use today, but may have a few items labelled as being rare, archaic, or literary. Thus the entry for *frosty* in the current edition of the *Oxford Thesaurus of English*[11] lists *freezing*, *frigid*, *glacial*, and *arctic* among the general terms, but also the literary word *frore*[12], and the rare adjectives *gelid*, *brumal*. The *Historical Thesaurus of the Oxford English Dictionary*, published (after forty-five years' work) in 2009,[13] does, as its name implies, offer words from all centuries. Consultation of an entry allows the user to discover which words were available to writers and speakers across the centuries. Ways of expressing the notion 'very cold' (not all of which survive today) have included:

frosty	late Middle English
frory	sixteenth century
frigidious	seventeenth century
Siberian	eighteenth century
arctic	nineteenth century
freezy	nineteenth century

Should it be allowed?

Whatever dictionary or language reference resource we use, the message is the same: we need to understand clearly what it offers. A news story which surfaced at the end of December 2009 illustrated the difficulties of confusion in this area—especially when there is disagreement as to what 'the dictionary' should contain. Headlines for the story included 'Are Scrabble's men of letters unfair to their Facebook counterparts?' (*Times*, 30 December 2009) and 'Facebook Scrabble dictionary angers expert players' (*Daily Mail*, 29 December 2009).

The background story, given here and in other papers, was of what the *Daily Mail* called a 'war' which had 'erupted among

Scrabble players'. In the traditional board game, words are authorized (or not) by the rules of the game, and by reference to an official Scrabble dictionary, which since 2003 has been the *Collins English Dictionary*.[14] Traditionally, categories such as proper nouns and foreign words have been regarded as unacceptable. However, it had become apparent that internet versions of the game (including an application available on the Facebook site) were consulting wordlists with a much wider remit: offending items highlighted in the news story were *et* as the past tense of 'eat', regarded as non-standard, *Iliad* (a proper name), French *moi* (a borrowing regarded as non-naturalized), *Pernod* (a trademark term), and *smoyle* (an archaic variant of 'smile').

The question here is not whether it would be possible for a dictionary to make a case for the inclusion of some or all of the disputed words. The interest lies in the illustration the story provides of the passions likely to be roused when conflicting versions of '*the* dictionary' collide.

Chapter 2
Unlocking the Wordhoard: exploring dictionary elements

As the previous chapter may suggest, the simplest answer to a question about a word could well be, *look it up in a good dictionary*. Certainly the standard 'building-blocks' of a traditional dictionary entry, such as spelling, pronunciation, origin, date, register, and meaning, offer us a variety of routes through which we can approach a word. A dictionary is therefore likely to be the first port of call in our voyage of exploration, and this chapter examines in detail the kind of systematic information a dictionary is likely to offer.

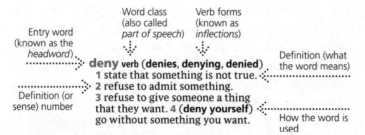

Exploded entry from the *Compact Oxford English Dictionary*, 3rd edn, showing typical features of a dictionary entry.

How do you say it?

Pronunciation may be indicated in several ways (depending on the size of the dictionary, and how much space it can afford, and judges necessary for a particular word). In a book where space is at a premium, full pronunciations may be limited to words where there is likely to be a difficulty. Some words—for example, monosyllables where there is no obvious alternative pronunciation—will be given without comment. Some will have a mark showing where the main stress falls on the word. In other cases, however, a full pronunciation may be given.

There are two main systems for this. One is what is known as 'respelling'. In this system (generally used in American dictionaries), a word will be spelt out again in accordance with a specified phonetic system. The other way (now favoured in British dictionaries) is to use the phonetic symbols of the International Phonetic Alphabet (IPA).

One natural response to an unfamiliar word (encountered through the written language) is to ask how it is pronounced—but the question makes the assumption that there is a single answer. In fact, as illustrated by Ira Gershwin's 'You like to-mato and I like to-mah-to',[1] we recognize readily that there may be more than one answer, depending on what regional variety of English we speak. Even within the same form there may be variation: the *Oxford Dictionary of English* offers three possible pronunciations for *garage* (noun), depending on stress or the sound of the final syllable. Exploration of the pronunciation history of a word can also be fruitful: lines in poetry of the eighteenth and early nineteenth century demonstrate that, for the verse in question to scan, *balcony* must once have been pronounced with the stress on the second syllable: for example in the following stanza of a poem of Byron's.

> And like so many Venuses of Titian's
> (The best's at Florence—see it, if ye will),
> They look when leaning over the balcony,
> Or stepp'd from out a picture by Giorgione.
> —Lord Byron *Beppo: a Venetian Story* (1818)

Some pronunciations survive only in literature of the past which is still read today. Others may be altered to generate related words: the dance term *chassé* has given us the less formal *sashay*. Sometimes we find that a version originally considered (and criticized) as incorrect is on its way to at least some degree of accepted status: *nuclear/nucular*[2] is an example of this. When considering pronunciation, we also might want to identify other words which offer a full rhyme, or which (like the word in which we are interested) continue to reflect the vowel-sounds and accentuation of another language.

Is that with a 'c'?

English spelling is, notoriously, less than transparent—something that language lovers often find a cause for celebration. As Philip Howard wrote in the *Times* of 20 October 2008, 'Spelling is verbal botany. We record the roots of words.' English spelling today may give you clues about the history of the word: in particular, what language it came from.[3] The spelling of the word *bureau* indicates its French origin. If we see words ending in *–ate* or *–ious*, we know that they are likely to reach back to Latin. The first syllable of *alcohol* and *algebra* reflects the Arabic definite article *al*, and allows us if we wish to investigate the second element of each word for further meaning. (The second element of *alcohol*, for instance, comes from the same Arabic word, *kuḥl*, which also gives us the eye make-up *kohl*. The earliest use of *alcohol* in English was to mean a powder, particularly kohl; in the seventeenth century, the word was extended to mean 'a distilled or rectified spirit', giving us the meaning we are familiar with today.) The information to which the spelling of the word has led may not be essential to our understanding of the bare meaning of the word in English today, but it adds richly to its interest.

Not everyone, however, is an enthusiast for the historical record as maintained in this way. In nineteenth-century America, the great lexicographer Noah Webster (1758–1843) was a pioneer in recommending and using a reformed system of spelling which dropped silent letters: for example, *music* instead of *musick* (now standard in English worldwide), and *honor* instead of *honour* (now standard in American English).

2008 was the centenary year for the foundation of the Simplified Spelling Society (established with the support of George Bernard Shaw). Ken Smith, a criminologist from Buckingham University, suggested in the *Times Higher Education Supplement* that it was time to accept common misspellings as variants rather than to correct them. A subsequent article in the *Economist* for August 2008 opened:

> Ghoti and tchoghs may not immediately strike readers as staples of the British diet … Yet the spelling, easily derived from other words, highlights the shortcomings of English orthography.
> —in *Economist* 14 August 2008

lexicographer

exicographer (like *lexicon*) comes through Latin from the Greek *lexikon biblion* 'book of words', and goes back ultimately to *lexis* meaning 'phrase, word, diction', from *legein* 'to speak'. The second element of the word represents the suffix *–graphy*, and comes from Greek *–graphia* writing, so a 'lexicographer' is someone who writes dictionaries.

The first dictionaries of English date from the seventeenth century, and the *OED*'s first example of *lexicographer* in use in English is dated 1658. Since that time, as more and more dictionaries have appeared, the word has become a familiar one, although not all references to the role are encouraging. In 1860 Lord Macaulay warned that 'The best lexicographer may well be content if his productions are received by the world with cold esteem.' And Dr Johnson's definition of *lexicographer* in his *Dictionary* (1755) is still famous: 'A writer of dictionaries; a harmless drudge.'

[A footnote to the opening phrase gave the key: *ghoti* spells *fish* with *gh* pronounced as in *tough*, *o* as in *women*, *ti* as in *nation*. *Tchoghs* equates to *chips* with *tch* as in *match*, *o* as in *women*, and *gh* as in *hiccough*.]

However, the columnist, while admitting the difficulty, went on to cite the warning of Mari Jones of Cambridge University that introducing phonetic spelling might involve choosing one regional variation over others as the 'norm', and would need frequent updating to reflect changes in pronunciation. Exploration of the spelling variants recorded for a single word may not only open up for us the current diversity of English spelling, but also give us an outline of how the current consensus was reached.

23

Where does it come from?

The question 'Where does it come from?' is one of the most likely enquiries to be made about a word. This continuing lay interest in word origins was perhaps highlighted by a report in the *Tulsa World* of 8 November 2008 on a notably overdue library book. The book in question was *New Word Analysis: or School Etymology of English Derivative Words*. Checked out at Holland Hall School in 1947, it had just been sent back to the library by the borrower (with a cheque for $250 to cover the intervening 61 years).

While this is likely to be an unusual case, interest in the origin of words is widespread. We may ask questions about the language of origin of a borrowed word, or about what etymologically close relations a word could have. A term may (as with *bandersnatch*[4]) have been consciously coined by an individual. Some items of vocabulary may derive from a misunderstanding, changed pronunciation, or alteration of spelling, which has gained sufficient exposure to have established its own individual identity.

Exploration of etymology can give us a picture of the descent of a word in current daily use. To take one example, the word *budget* (from Old French *bougette*, a diminutive form of *bouge* 'leather bag', from Latin *bulga* 'leather bag, knapsack') originally meant a pouch or wallet, and later also its contents. In the mid eighteenth century, the Chancellor of the Exchequer, in presenting his annual statement, was said 'to open the budget'. By the following century, the term had moved from government to cover other finances. We can also gain access to a wider picture by looking for other words from the same source: in this instance, *bulge* which in Middle English meant 'wallet or bag', and in the early seventeenth century 'a ship's bilge', also comes ultimately from Latin *bulga*. The current sense with which we are familiar, 'a rounded swelling that distorts an otherwise flat surface', and which developed later, presumably derives from association with the shape of a full bag.

A number of famous 'etymologies' (such as the suggestion that the adjective *posh* derives from the initial letters of *Port Out, Starboard Home*[5]) have been demonstrated to be without foundation. They are, however, more interesting than simple error: they may reflect popular notions of social and cultural history. It can be of interest to explore how long a particular belief has been current, and what conflicting explanations for the same word can be found.

When was it first used?

To ask when a particular word first appeared in the language is one of the most basic questions, and may be a difficult one to answer. With a word that has already been recorded we are likely to have a date of first use[6]: that is, the earliest recorded use that we know of for that particular word. In some cases, of course, we really do know the coinage. *Bandersnatch*, for example, was coined by Lewis Carroll in 1871, as a name for a mythical creature in *Through the Looking-Glass*. *Banoffi* was invented by Nigel Mackenzie, proprietor of the Hungry Monk restaurant in Jevington, Sussex, where *banoffi pie* with its sliced bananas and soft toffee was first served in 1972.

Bandersnatch and *banoffi* are striking words, and we do not find it surprising that they emerged from an individual creation.

In other cases, a word may seem so familiar, such a part of the mainstream language, that we might assume that there is nothing very interesting to say about its origin. A word like *scientist*, however, confounds this view. Investigation reveals not only its date of first use, but that it emerged after considerable discussion. The *Quarterly Review* of 1834 gave an account of the discussions prompted by the realization of 'the want of any name' by which 'students of the knowledge of the material world' could be designated collectively.

> *Philosophers* was felt to be too wide and lofty a term, and was very properly forbidden them by Mr Coleridge, both in his capacity as philologer and metaphysician; *savans* was rather assuming, besides being French instead of English; some ingenious gentleman proposed that, by analogy with *artist*, they might form *scientist*.
> —in *Quarterly Review* 1834, vol. 51

We might think that the suggestion was so obviously right as to be greeted with acclaim, but that was not how things were seen in 1834. Noting that the proposed term 'was not generally palatable', the *Quarterly Review* continued:

> Others attempted to translate the term by which members of similar associations in Germany have described themselves, but it was not found easy to discover an English equivalent for *natur-forscher*. The process of examination which it implies might suggest such undignified compounds as *nature-poker*, or *nature-peeper*, for these *naturae curiosi*, but these were indignantly rejected.
> —in *Quarterly Review* 1834, vol. 51

It is not on the whole surprising that *scientist* triumphed, but it is worth noting how widely a simple question about the date of first use has taken us. We have not only discovered the principle on which the word was formed (analogy with an existing term), we have had a glimpse of the rejected alternatives, and the tense discussion surrounding the whole topic.

First use, of course, is only one approach to linguistic dating. We may want to know whether a particular word or sense existed in or survived to or into a given century. The June 2009 quarterly revision of the *OED* made available online included a detailed analysis of the development of the word *recession*, confirming that it was not until the early twentieth century that the sense which economic events of 2009 made painfully recognizable became part of our vocabulary.

Who uses it?

Many items of vocabulary come from a particular area of usage, perhaps belonging to a group linked by region or interest: dialect and slang are two obvious examples. However, even apparently obscure terms may suddenly catch the public notice. The late William Safire drew attention to a particular form of this occurrence in September 2007: 'Every few years, Senator Orrin Hatch, Republican of Utah, startles the Senate by bringing back an obscure Americanism.' Examples cited were *hissy fit* (1996) and *canoodler* (1998). In 2007, according to Safire, Hatch produced 'an even more archaic resuscitation of an imaginative Americanism'. This was *absquatulation* (meaning the action of absconding), as used in a Virginia newspaper during the American Civil War. Safire concluded:

> Hatch made the Senate rafters ring with his speech this summer warning colleagues that 'our enemies will be

> emboldened' by withdrawal from Iraq, concluding on
> this historically reverberating note: 'Mr President, abs-
> quatulation is not a policy!'
>
> —William Safire in *New York Times* 2 September 2007

In November 2008, contributions to the *Times* letter pages welcomed the use of *claggy* in a cookery column, claiming it variously as Lincolnshire and Northumberland usage. As one correspondent wrote:

> The term 'claggy' is still current on Tyneside. Last week,
> at the Laing Art Gallery in Newcastle, I enjoyed creating,
> with my four-year-old granddaughter, a paper mosaic
> pattern using scissors and paste.
> Or, as I taught her to say, 'cut and clag'.
>
> —letter in *Times* 6 November 2008

Stories of this kind remind us that words of more limited currency may suddenly appear in mainstream use, constituting starting-points for further exploration[7]. On the other hand, we may come across a term from an earlier period or specific region through pursuing our own interests. Many people today enjoy researching their family history, and this may well mean that they need to decode an occupational term (often, from an industry which is now defunct, or where practices have changed with changing technology), or perhaps the name of the illness given as the cause of someone's death. To take one example, a reference to *consumption* today is likely to trigger thoughts of *conspicuous consumption*, or the *consumer society*. We are less likely to think of what was once a dominant sense: *consumption* as the name of a wasting disease, in particular pulmonary tuberculosis.

What does it mean?

While 'What does it mean?' is one of the most basic questions to ask about a word, the answer (as previous sections have already indicated) can be far from straightforward. Many words have more than one sense, and the correct answer may be affected by the date of the usage which is being decoded, or the context in which it appears. Today, if asked the meaning of the word *computer*, most people would respond with a version of the definition in the *Oxford Dictionary of English*:

> An electronic device which is capable of receiving information (data) in a particular form and of performing a sequence of operations in accordance with a predetermined but variable set of procedural instructions (program) to produce a result in the form of information or signals.
>
> —*Oxford Dictionary of English* (2nd edn revised, 2005)

This dominant sense developed during the second half of the twentieth century (and in its first occurrences, as the revised *Oxford English Dictionary* points out, is not easily distinguishable from the older meaning of 'A device or machine capable of performing or facilitating calculation', first recorded in 1869). However, the word is much older than that: between the early seventeenth and the mid nineteenth centuries *computer* meant 'a person who makes calculations or computations'. This is the sense of Jonathan Swift's reference in *A Tale of a Tub* (1704) to 'A very skillful Computer, who hath given a full Demonstration of it from Rules of Arithmetick.'

As the example of *budget* given in the previous section has already demonstrated, exploration of the sense development of a word may take the reader through a series of steps. *Shambles* meaning 'a state of total disorder' derives immediately from the earlier sense of 'a butcher's slaughterhouse', and goes back ultimately to the medieval *shamble* in the singular as 'a stall for the sale of meat', and finally to the Old English word for 'stool'.

Budget and *shambles* show sense development over centuries, but of course language change is a constant process. It is possible to pick up on changes of meaning happening in our own time, often through technological development. Print dictionaries of 2009 would have had meanings for *twitter* and *tweet* relating to the chirping of young birds, or light and trivial talk. For many of their readers (as revised and updated editions in hard copy or online will in due course show), the first sense that currently comes immediately to mind is likely to relate to the text-based posts of *Twitter*, trademark name of the popular social networking and microblogging service. Even many of those who did not at the time post *tweets* would have been made more aware of this form of communication by accounts of the use made of Twitter by youthful opposition supporters in Iran, following the presidential election, and subsequent government crackdown, of June 2009.

In the longer view, it will of course remain to be seen whether the sense continues to be dominant, or whether—as technology moves on—the usage will be left as an interesting footnote to the linguistic and technological history of the twenty-first century.

What else does a dictionary tell us?

So far in this chapter, we have looked at the main areas of information in a typical dictionary entry. However, to ensure that we get all we can out of our chosen resource, there are other points we need to consider.

A dictionary entry for a single word may contain information about a number of other lexical items: for example, phrases in which the word appears, or words which have been derived from the headword by the addition of one of the standard suffixes. For example, an entry for the word *twitter* might have the phrase *in a twitter* as an informal expression meaning 'in a state of excitement', and the derivatives *twitterer* and *twittery*.

Many words will have long sections of compounds or phrases, although with current dictionaries it is increasingly the practice to give well-established and much-used compounds their own headword status. An entry for *golden*, for example, will be followed by separate entries (in alphabetic sequence) for key compounds such as *golden age*, *golden calf*, *golden handshake*, *Golden Horde*, and *golden rule*.

The accordance (where space allows) of separate-entry status is more user-friendly, part of an increasing awareness on the part of dictionary makers of the requirements of their users. Earlier dictionaries (in this as in other ways) were likely to make more demands upon their readers, requiring them to read carefully through columns and pages of closely-printed text to find the item they wanted. However, given that alphabetizing follows strict letter-by-letter rules, we need to remember that not all the compounds belonging to a particular word will follow it without interruption. Thus if we are looking for compounds beginning with the word *gold*, we need to remember that *golden* and its compounds will intervene between *gold digger* and *goldfinch*.

Making sense of the dictionary

Having looked at the main building-blocks of a dictionary entry, it is appropriate to consider overall organization. Words are, as we have already noted, given in strict alphabetical order of entries. Words which have exactly the same spelling, but a different meaning and origin (known as homonyms or homographs) are distinguished as separate entries with a superscript number.

Within an entry, main senses are separated, and it is at this point that it is particularly important to be aware of whether you are looking at a dictionary of the historical language, or one which focuses on the language of today. If it is the former, the senses will be ordered chronologically: that is, the first sense you see will be the earliest recorded sense. With major historical dictionaries such as the *Oxford English Dictionary* and the *Shorter Oxford English Dictionary*, the first sense may well be one which has been obsolete for centuries. If you are looking for what appears to be a mainstream word of today, a current dictionary is the first place to look. Here senses will be ordered according to usage: the sense which evidence shows to be the primary one will come first. To go back to one of the words we looked at earlier in the chapter, the first sense in *SOED* for *budget* is 'a pouch or wallet', dating from late Middle English and labelled as obsolete except for dialect usage. The first sense in the *Oxford Dictionary of English* (2nd edn) is 'an estimate of income and expenditure for a set period of time'. The earlier meaning of 'a pouch or wallet' has been placed in the etymology, as an important part of its history.

wordhoard

In May 2009, a column on the website of a digital marketing agency, discussing the revival of the written word through such online resources as texting, Facebook, and Twitter, was headed 'Logging in: Unlocking the Wordhoard'. The heading brings together two very different worlds: the technologically developed world of today, and Anglo-Saxon England.

'Unlocking the Wordhoard' presents us with two possibilities for exploration: *wordhoard* as a compound, or the longer phrase of which it is a part. If we take the second option, and search online, we need to think about how to frame the search. If what we have is an example of a phrase which might be rendered *unlock the wordhoard* or *unlock your wordhoard*, we need a catch-all search. Putting the two expressions 'unlock' and 'word hoard' into the search engine returns a whole range of possibilities, including advertisements for 'Beowulf Word Hoard' T-shirts and bags, decorated with the words *wordhord onleac* and the name *Beowulf*.

With this clue, we can go back to accounts of the great Anglo-Saxon poem, and find that for someone to 'unlock their wordhoard' was to make a formal speech. Today, it is a phrase that still has life for us, perhaps because we are so aware of the treasury of words available to us.

Chapter 3
The Art of Interrogation: what questions to ask

I N the previous chapter, we looked at ways in which we can make best use of what dictionaries offer us through their systematic organization of material. Keeping such areas as origin, spelling, date, pronunciation, and meaning in mind, it is now time to look in more detail at the kinds of question we may want to ask.

'What does it mean?' is an obvious, and straightforward, question, but it may be only a beginning. A word may have more than one sense. It might have meant something very different in the past, and it could already be on the move: beginning to develop a sense which will become established in the future. Questions about meaning can focus on past, present, or future.

Sensitivity to usage can extend to other areas. We can be alert to the circumstances in which a word appears. Are there indications (quotation marks, or perhaps a qualifying expression like 'so called') which suggest that the person using the word is not fully confident that it will be recognized and understood? And what is the reason for the hesitancy: is it felt that the word in question is now passing out of use, or is it being tagged as a new coinage which has hardly settled down, and which may be ephemeral?

Couth, kempt, and shevelled

On the death of the jazz musician Johnny Dankworth in February 2010, more than one affectionate obituary quoted an assessment of his music (attributed to the writer and musician Kitty Grime) as having been 'couth, kempt and shevelled'. Consideration of this phrase can open up several points about word origins.

Most obviously, the three words *couth*, *kempt*, and *shevelled* are 'positives' generated by removing the first syllables of the negative adjectives *uncouth*, *unkempt*, and *dishevelled*. In order to know what we are dealing with, the first step will be to look up each word: do *couth*, *kempt*, and *shevelled* have mainstream life of their own? (A pointer to their being less than established is found in the *Times* obituary, in which they appear as *'couth*, *'kempt*, and *'shevelled*, with the use of an apostrophe to indicate the loss of an expected prefix.) And what might the etymologies for *uncouth*, *unkempt*, and *dishevelled* tell us? The results are interesting for the light they throw on our particular phrase.

Of the first three terms we are looking at, *couth* with the meaning 'refined, well-mannered' goes back to the late nineteenth century, and was formed by dropping the prefix *un-* from *uncouth* (in what is called technically a 'back-formation'). However, if we explore a little further, and consult a dictionary which covers the historical language as well as the usage familiar today, we find that this is not the whole picture. *Couth* meaning 'known' dates back to Old English, and was current until the seventeenth century. It has had a separate life in Scots, with the meaning 'kind, agreeable' recorded from the medieval period, and 'comfortable, cosy' from the eighteenth century.

The humorous creation in the late nineteenth century of a word to mean the opposite of *uncouth* was simply the latest chapter in a much longer story.

Kempt is in some ways more straightforward, since its meaning of 'neat and clean' has not changed greatly. However, it is also a word which repays a little extra attention. It goes back to Old English, and comes from a verb related to *comb*: the implication here is that initially the neat state it denotes was achieved by combing. Again, a dictionary which specializes in the historical language gives us a little more. For a substantial part of its life, *kempt* was applied to hair or wool that had been combed or neatly brushed and trimmed. It was then extended to describe someone (or something) characterized by looking tidy and well-cared-for.

The third member of the trio, *shevelled*, is in some ways the most interesting. It is probably not surprising that it does not (unlike *couth* and *kempt*) appear in dictionaries of either the current or the historical language. It is, therefore, much more of an off-the-cuff creation, to bring it into line with the other two terms. However, when we look more closely, this again is not the whole story.

It is not of course difficult to find its origin: *dishevelled* is a reasonably well-known word, and could anyway be deduced: *'shevelled* has clearly dropped a first (negative) element, and *dis-* comes naturally to mind. However, when we examine the word from which it comes, we find a more complex picture. *Dishevelled*, which dates from the medieval period, originally meant 'having the hair uncovered or hanging loose'; subsequently, this came to mean 'untidy'. If we look at the elements of which it is made up, we can see it has two parts: the prefix *dis-*, and the second element which ultimately comes from an Old French word *chevel*, meaning 'hair'. The creation of *shevelled*, while fun and (in context) immediately explicable, has left us with a term in which only part of the original prefix might seem to have been lost: the final *s* of *dis-* has been retained.

In fact, this is not a case of what is called 'misdivision', in which a word's development depends on misunderstanding of elements. In this case, the *sh-* of *shevelled* can be seen as equating to the *ch-* of *chevel*. However, speculation about the point does bring up a particular type of word development, and might encourage an interested person to look for other examples.[1]

Seven Portugal onions

We may come across indications of a thread to pursue at any point. In the early 1980s, when work on the *Supplement* to the *Oxford English Dictionary* had reached the letter P, I was reading a story of Kipling's on the bus on my way into work. In the story, 'Fairy-Kist', I came across the following passage. The narrator is describing a conversation at a dinner with friends:

> Burges told us how an illustrious English astrologer called
> Lily had once erected a horoscope to discover the where-
> abouts of a parcel of stolen fish. The stars led him straight
> to it and the thief and, incidentally, into a breeze with a
> lady over 'seven Portugal onions'.
> —Rudyard Kipling 'Fairy-Kist' in *Limits and Renewals* (1932)

The quotation marks around 'seven Portugal onions' were an immediate prompt. When I checked the existing *OED*,

Twitterati

In February 2010, the headline of a Press Association release, '"Twitterati" want rocker in Senate', highlighted the enthusiasm of the online community using Twitter to persuade the US rocker John Mellencamp to run for the Senate. Apart from underscoring the degree to which *Twitter* is now a part of everyone's vocabulary, whether or not they themselves use it, the term also prompts questions about its formation. There is (as yet) no suffix *–ati* listed in dictionaries, so the assumption must be that it is formed on the model of another word: *glitterati*.

Exploration of this reveals a process of word formation that can go a further step. *Glitterati*, an informal name for the set of fashionable people engaged in glamorous activities such as show business, emerged in the 1950s, and at that time would have had just the flavour of up-to-dateness that *Twitterati* has today. It emerged from a blend of *glitter* and *literati:* a seventeenth-century term (from Latin) meaning 'well-educated people who are interested in literature'.

The accidental rhyming of *Twitter* and *glitter* allowed the latest coinage: it remains to be seen whether one day, through the process of language change, new words with different stems will be formed on a new suffix of *–ati* or *–erati*.

I found that *Portugal onion* was listed, but there was no usage evidence for it.[2] It looked worth investigating, and the reference to 'an illustrious English astrologer' offered a promising lead. The astrologer in question seemed likely to be the seventeenth-century astrologer William Lilly (1602–81). As there was no indication of a specific source, I decided to try to cut down the odds by looking in a book which I knew was familiar to

Kipling: Isaac D'Israeli's *Curiosities of Literature* (1791–1823). I found there an article on 'English Astrologers' which had a lively account of Lilly (D'Israeli called him 'this arch rogue'). Although I did not find the anecdote I wanted, there was a reference to one of Lilly's books, *Christian Astrology*, which sounded worth a try.

Skimming through the book I found the story I wanted. Lilly, who was living in the country, had bought some fish in London, which was to come down by barge. However, there was a robbery at the warehouse in which his fish was stored. The fish was taken, together with a bag belonging to the water-man who should have delivered the fish to Lilly.

Turning to his special expertise, Lilly used a horoscope to identify the thief and locate the missing goods. However, when they traced the fish they found it had been partially eaten, and that was not the only reason to complain:

> The thiefe stole the bag as well as the fish; the barge-man, whose sack it was ... said to the woman of the house, Woman, so I may have my sack which I lost last night, I care not ... I as heavily complained to the woman for seven Portugall Onyons which I lost; she not knowing what they were, made pottage with them.
> —William Lilly *Christian Astrology* (1647)

'Portugal onion' was a name for a large mild-flavoured variety of onion, which passed out of use in the nineteenth century. William Lilly's story is (to date) still the earliest example we have of the term, so following up the reference found by accident was well worth while, as well as enjoyable. It revealed a colourful story, and incidentally validated the original decision to include the term. Portugal onions had been with us for longer than the evidence available in the early 1900s might have suggested.

Beyond the dictionary?

A dictionary entry for a specific word may be packed with information, but it cannot give us the whole story. The typical dictionary entry is based on assumptions about what the user needs to know. Constrictions of space mean that the information is likely to be provided in highly concentrated form, and properly limited to what are regarded as lexicographical essentials: spelling, pronunciation, meaning, immediate origin, and perhaps date of introduction. The smaller the dictionary, the more concentrated the entry, as the history of the word *telegraphese* indicates.

In a world of texting and tweeting, telegrams seem to be part of a more leisured age—but there was a time when they were a product of the cutting edge of technology, and they gave their name to a form of highly compressed language which impinged on the dictionary world.

Dictionaries today are consciously user-friendly, balancing constrictions of extent with a desire to produce readable definitions which do not make unreasonable demands upon the reader, but in earlier days, smaller dictionaries at least were less indulgent. *Telegraphese* in the sense 'the terse, abbreviated style of language used in telegrams' dates back to 1885 (the *Pall Mall Gazette* predicted 'We shall gradually give up English in favour of Telegraphese'), and by 1911 it appeared in the Preface to the first edition of the *Concise Oxford Dictionary*. The Editors (H. W. Fowler and his brother) were clearly concerned to warn their readers of the necessary effects of concision to ensure that their dictionary provided as much essential information as possible:

> If common words are to be treated at length, and their uses to be copiously illustrated, space must be saved both by the curtest possible treatment of all that are either uncommon or fitter for the encyclopaedia than the dictionary, and by the severest economy of expression— amounting to the adoption of telegraphese—that readers can be expected to put up with.
> —H. W. and F. G. Fowler (eds) *Concise Oxford Dictionary*, 1907, Preface, p. iii

The Fowlers, by an oversight that any lexicographer can sympathize with, did not in fact include *telegraphese* in their dictionary: it had to be added at a later stage. Today it is a term likely to appear, but the style it denotes has largely vanished from dictionary pages.

While the main elements of a dictionary entry (as shown in the previous chapter) can all offer excellent starting points for exploration, there are other ways in which we can approach a word in order to find out more of its story. It is at this point that we can begin to set our own limits, deciding what it is about a word that we want to know. We may choose to see the word that interests us as a member of a particular set. In November 2009, the magazine *Women's Wear Daily* posted an online interview with the model Kate Moss, which included the following exchange:

> WWD: Do you have a motto?
> KM: There are loads. There's 'Nothing tastes as good as

skinny feels.' That's one of them. You try and remember,
but it never works.
—in *Women's Wear Daily* (www.wwd.com) 13 November
2009

The exchange provoked a furore, polarized between *Female First's* characterization of her response as 'jaw-dropping' and the British politician Lembit Opik's comment in the *Sun* newspaper that the statement underlined 'everything that is wrong with the fashion world' on the one hand, and a *Times* column headed 'Lighten up—Kate Moss is right' on the other. The debate here, of course, is on the question of weight loss and maintenance in the context of health, but those interested in language might pause to consider the vocabulary used. What synonyms can be identified for *skinny*? And which of them (including Moss's word of choice) have typically been used with positive connotations?

A first step here would be to think of other words in our own vocabulary. Moss's response might have awoken the echo of a comment attributed to the Duchess of Windsor, 'You can never be too rich or too thin', and *thin* is an obvious starting point. Recourse to a thesaurus offers a range of further terms under this heading, with one group under *slim* offering *lean, slender, willowy, svelte*, and *sylphlike*, and a second under *skinny* including *underweight, scrawny, scraggy, bony*, and *gaunt*.

The implication of these groupings is that *skinny* has typically been used in a critical way to describe a body shape in which thinness has gone beyond elegance to look undernourished and underweight—below what is expected or desirable—and this is supported by current dictionary definitions. They include

'unattractively thin' (*Oxford Dictionary of English*), 'lacking sufficient flesh: very thin' (*Merriam-Webster's Collegiate Dictionary*),
and 'lacking in flesh; thin' (*Collins English Dictionary*). The *Oxford
English Dictionary* confirms that this sense goes back to the early
seventeenth century, in the description of the Weird Sisters in
Macbeth:

> Each at once her choppy finger laying
> Upon her skinny lips.
> —Shakespeare *Macbeth* (1606), act 1, sc. 3

It is not until the twenty-first century that the evidence provided suggests a positive context, in an assertion (presumably
by a former model) from *Cosmopolitan* magazine: 'When I was
starting out, you had to be waif-thin, and I was never skinny
enough.'

Are there other contexts in which the word is seen as
more positive? The answer seems to be, yes, at least by implication, in the mid-twentieth-century informal use of *skinny*
to denote coffee made with skimmed or semi-skimmed
milk.[3]

Returning to the definitions of *skinny* as applied to body
mass, it is notable that they all include the word *thin*. Consultation of definitions for this word offer 'having little, or too little,
flesh or fat on the body' (*Oxford Dictionary of English*[4]), 'not
well fleshed: lean' (*Merriam-Webster's Collegiate Dictionary*[5]),
and 'slim or lean' (*Collins English Dictionary*[6]). We can take it
that *thin* is, on the whole, a neutral term, and one of which
words like *skinny* and *slim* are subsets. However, it has not necessarily been taken as particularly complimentary, despite the
Duchess of Windsor.

One way of exploring this further is to see how it is used in expressions of the 'thin as a—' construction. Professional lexicographers, or dictionary writers, would turn at this point to corpus material: for example, the Oxford Corpus, developed by Oxford University Press as a major resource for their dictionaries. A corpus as defined here is 'a collection of texts of written (or spoken) language presented in electronic form', providing evidence of real-life language use. Analysis of corpus evidence allows lexicographers to see the typical contexts in which particular words are used.[7] Even the amateur word enthusiast may have access to this kind of resource: as described in the following chapter, the British National Corpus (BNC) and the Corpus of Contemporary American English (COCA) are both freely available. It is also possible to apply the process of sifting lexical evidence to the mass of material more widely available through the World Wide Web.

To avoid being overwhelmed with material, it is sensible to limit the files being searched by date: to take a snapshot of the language for the current year only. A search of Google News in November 2009 for the string 'thin as a' produced between three and four hundred hits. Scanning by eye eliminated a number which did not refer to human body mass (for example, a flat loudspeaker was described as 'thin as a sheet of foil'). Relevant items gathered were:

thin as a bean shoot
thin as a blade of grass [or bluegrass]
thin as a bone
thin as a broom
thin as a cigarette

thin as a greyhound
thin as a horsehair
thin as a kipper
thin as a lizard
thin as a pin
thin as a pinstripe
thin as a pipe cleaner
thin as a pole
thin as a rail
thin as a rake
thin as a reed
thin as a rope
thin as a scarecrow
thin as a skewer
thin as a snooker cue
thin as a stick
thin as a straw
thin as a supermodel
thin as a ten-year-old
thin as a twig
thin as a whip
thin as a whippet

Of these, easily the most popular words for comparison were *rail* (26), *rake* (11), *reed* (7), and *stick* (8): all words which refer to something which typifies a straight, narrow shape. Also popular, and more colourfully, we have *supermodel* (6), and *whippet* (4)[8]. Other terms occur only once: for example, *blade of bluegrass* and *skewer*.

With the exception of *scarecrow*, the objects chosen for comparison are not obviously unflattering. Exploring context more

Corpus: **new_oec_plus_biwec**
Hits: **40**
conc description | Report a bug

Home | Concordance | Word List | Word Sketch | Thesaurus | Sketch-Diff
View options | Sample | Filter | Sort | Frequency | Collocation | Save

Page 1 ▼ of 2 Go   Next | Last

arts	untouchable source of invaluable information . Thin **as a** pole . he looks every bit the dodgy underworld
computing	function user interfaces . Not quite as thin **as a** 'network computer' , after all , network
computing	Fish . The system builds parts in layers as thin **as a** thousandth of an inch , and can " draw
fiction	enough , whatever it was . I see ! You 're thin **as a** rail ! Haynath will skin us both if you
life_and_leisure	waistband . Cute but only if you 're as thin **as a** mannequin . </p><p> The Mini No explanation
life_and_leisure	town makes a better grilled pizza crust - thin **as a** bad excuse and crisp as the unforgiving
life_and_leisure	It 's strange , because my sister was as thin **as a** stick and now she 's larger than me . Sara-Jane
life_and_leisure	big and my face is too small my body is thin **as a** clarinet and my ankles are so skinny that
news	are you striving to be as unrealistically thin **as a** supermodel ? One good way to find out is
news	Ethiopian Kebede may be 24 - but it 's thin **as a** bar girl 's promise . This will be a blowout
news	not weighing 8 stone . Her mother is as thin **as a** pin . Fiona wanted children you have to
news	should not be 14 - stone . He should be thin **as a** rake . ' It 's a cruel , cruel twist of
news	with Solano of Peru and Kieron Dwyer , both thin **as a** pencil but twice as sharp , causing panic
news	's short , receding , sallow-skinned and thin **as a** rake ! " The first time we meet is at a
society	grow out of it - and he did . Now he 's as thin **as a** beanpole . I 'm sure if he 'd dieted be
society	ightower , whose Lone Star folksiness has worn thin **as a** roadkill rattler on the Waco highway ,
sport	dropped . During that time he became as thin **as a** stick insect . For a while , he stopped
weblog	of the International Basketball League . Thin **as a** pipe cleaner , Samake led the IBL in blocked
weblog	person overall than who I was when I was thin **as a** rail . But why can't we have it all ? </p>
	between me and where I am . It can be as thin **as a** piece of sail cloth put up for a tent ;

Page 1 ▼ of 2 Go   Next | Last

Corpus search for *thin* showing key word in context

fully, we find references in which carrying no extra weight is seen as a sign of health and fitness, as for example in the description of a centenarian army veteran of the 1980s as having been 'thin as a rail, ramrod straight' (from the Letters page of the *Charlottesville Daily Progress*, online edition, 15 November 2009), or a former college room mate as having been 'thin as a rail, with a classic Byronic profile' (in www.newsobserver.com, 30 October 2009).

In other cases, the expression is used as part of a description of someone in poor physical health. At the beginning of November, the American website *The Drudge Report* carried a report which read:

> Eyebrows raised over the weekend as President Obama walked out of the gym at Fort McNair—appearing thin as a rail! Rigorous workouts and high-stress basketball games are said to be behind the dramatic weight loss.
> —in www.drudgereport.com 2 November 2009

Coverage of the ensuing debate takes us back to *skinny*. The week before the *Drudge Report* item appeared, the *New York Times* of 27 October 2009 had carried a report of a Democratic fund-raiser in Miami, at which the President had told his audience, 'Just because I'm skinny doesn't mean I'm not tough.' In the British press, the *Daily Mail*, summarizing the news coverage, wound up an article of 3 November 2009 with the words, 'The news that Mr Obama is skinny because he exercises will be welcomed by health professionals.'

Deciding what to ask

Any word can present a question, and each person will have their own approach to language, with their own particular

nucular

When Governor Sarah Palin exploded on to the stage of US national politics she became the subject of frenzied attention, and both positive and negative comment. One particular criticism centred on her pronunciation of 'nuclear': why, it was asked, did she pronounce it 'nucular'?

The pronunciation was taken by some as an indicator of ignorance, but investigation shows that, if deplored, it has a considerable history. The *Oxford English Dictionary* records *nucular* from 1943 as an alteration 'representing a colloquial pronunciation (widely criticized by usage guides)'. The *Merriam-Webster Collegiate*, while noting widespread disapproval, noted also widespread use among 'educated speakers including . . . at least two U.S. presidents and one vice president'.

Finally, a column by Steven Pinker in the *New York Times* in October 2008 concluded that, far from being a sign of ignorance, 'nucular' simply showed a common reversal of vowel-like consonants 'and is no more illiterate than pronouncing "iron" the way most Americans do, as "eye-yern" instead of "eye-ren"'.

The evidence overall suggests that *nucular* is a variant which will continue to attract, but to survive, criticism.

points of interest. However, when considering what we can usefully ask, it can be helpful to see where others have been before us. To take a couple of examples, the Oxford Dictionaries language site (www.oxforddictionaries.com) has a page for Frequently Asked Questions, listing some of the queries which have been sent in over the years. As well as a list of popular questions, from 'What is the longest English word?' to 'What is the origin of the dollar sign ($)?', readers can browse through the content of specific categories. If you select 'Spelling', 'Usage', or 'Word Origins', you will click through to a list of questions (and their answers) on the specific topic.

Michael Quinion's *World Wide Words* site (www.worldwidewords. org) has a 'Questions and Answers' section, in which articles based on questions about words and phrases are organized alphabetically according to the word or phrase concerned (from *a flea in one's ear* to *zilch*). Material like this has a double value: it may be that you will find your own specific question already answered, or you may find fresh ideas for exploration in a particular direction.

A word is known by the company it keeps

The same word can be grouped in a number of different ways. If we take *twitter* as an example, one category might be that of origin. While forms of the word ('cognates') exist in a number of different languages, the overall origin is imitative. The sound of the word is thought to resemble the light chirping of a bird. We could investigate what synonyms it has. We might decide that we wanted to look for other words of imitative origin, for example *caw* and *chirrup*. Alternatively, we might be interested in the way in which Twitter was seen by authorities in Iran, as a kind of subversive publishing. In that light, it could be grouped with the Russian word *samizdat* (the literal meaning of which is 'self-publishing house'), which in the days of the Cold War was used for the clandestine copying and circulation of literature which had been banned by the state. Or, we might be interested in words that rhyme with it (for one of them, *glitter*, see the panel on *Twitterati* on p. 39).

Famously said

So far we have considered ways in which we can investigate word origins and shades of meaning. Another approach would be to ask whether a particular word or phrase had been used in a notable context: perhaps it was used by a famous person, or in a well-known speech. A cue for investigating this kind of thing appeared in a *Times* leader of 23 March 2010. A lead news story of the day centred on allegations of bullying in Downing Street, and the *Times* first leader was headed (without explanation) 'Bully Pulpit'. Since this is a less than transparent phrase, a reader might understandably wonder why it had been used, and whether it indicated a play on words.

Recourse to a dictionary gives an immediate answer: the phrase *bully pulpit* is American, and is used for a public office or position of authority which allows its occupant to speak out on any issue. However, its origin adds something to the story: it was apparently used by President Theodore Roosevelt, when explaining his view of the presidency. A dictionary of quotations provides the precise wording: his gleeful statement (in 1909, the final year of his presidency) 'I have got such a bully pulpit!' The term passed into the language: nearly eighty years later, Nancy Reagan as First Lady quoted it when she said:

> If the President has a bully pulpit, then the First Lady has a white glove pulpit ... more refined, restricted, but it's a pulpit all the same.
> —Nancy Reagan in *New York Times* 10 March 1988

At this point, we have identified the origin of 'bully pulpit', but may well want to know exactly how the positive adjective in Roosevelt's expression is related to the much less favourable verb of the news story. The answer is quite complex: an example of how words shift their meaning. *Bully* was originally (in the sixteenth century) a term of endearment; it later became a familiar form of address to a male friend. It was not until the late seventeenth century that it developed the negative sense of someone who uses strength or position to intimidate another person, and the verb 'to bully' comes from that. However, the informal adjective *bully* in American English (meaning 'very good') developed from the earlier, positive sense of the noun.

If we go back to the world of quotations and sayings, we can find examples of all three meanings. We have already seen the Roosevelt usage. In Shakespeare's *Henry V*, the admiring soldiers say of the King:

> The king's a bawcock, and a heart of gold,
> A lad of life, an imp of fame,
> Of parents good, of fist most valiant:
> I kiss his dirty shoe, and from my heart-string
> I love the lovely bully.
> —Shakespeare *Henry V* (1599), act 4, sc. 1

On the other hand, the proverbial saying 'a bully is always a coward' is recorded from the early nineteenth century.

Getting ideas

We may have no shortage of questions to ask, and we may already have identified the particular area of language that interests us, from etymology to the introduction of new words. However, there is always the possibility that there is an approach we have not thought of. FAQs on dictionary and language websites may generate ideas, and the material made available round events like a national spelling bee can be similarly productive. Looking at what other people have asked, or at key tips that would-be top spellers are being offered, may trigger a new question in our own minds, or take us off down yet another linguistic path.

Putting the question

There is really no limit to the questions we can ask of words: the key point is to establish what interests us—and to be alert (as with the use of *bully pulpit*) when an interesting story may be concealed behind a word or phrase.

Chapter 4
The Art of Exploration (i): where to look for answers

ONCE we have identified the questions we want to ask, we need to move on to the art of exploration: where to look for the answers.[1]

Enquiring readers

The 'enquiring reader' was a familiar figure of nineteenth-century reference writing. In 1831, an advertisement in the *Edinburgh Journal* for John Timbs's *Knowledge for the People: or, the Plain Why and Because, Familiarizing Subjects of Useful Curiosity and Amusing Research: from the best and latest authorities* introduced this notable resource in the following words:

> The design of this work is to present the enquiring Reader with just so many useful enquiries and new facts, as may combine information with amusement: and gratify curiosity upon hundreds of laudable topics, without fatigue or uninviting study.
>
> —in *The Edinburgh Literary Journal* 7 May 1831

In 1860, the 'enquiring reader' appeared again in a review of Kenneth Mackenzie's edition of *The Marvellous Adventures and Rare Conceits of Master Tyll Owlglass*:

> Mr. Mackenzie's translation is at once racy and careful, and his management of the book throughout deserves our highest praise. His Preface and Appendixes are replete with curious matter, and there is no question, we think, that could possibly occur to the most enquiring reader which would not find its solution here.
>
> —in *The Gentleman's Magazine*, vol. 208, January 1860

In the twenty-first century, the 'enquiring reader' has probably never had a richer range of sources through which questions of language can be pursued, either in print or online. This chapter will look firstly at the type of English language dictionary resources available, in print and online, and then more widely at other reference works.

Turning the pages

Naturally enough, all our major English language dictionaries and related resources first appeared in hard copy. Some of them now look back a long way to their origins: the first part (A–ANT) of the *New English Dictionary*, now known as the *Oxford English Dictionary*, first appeared in 1884. One of the most recent publications, the two-volume *Historical Thesaurus of the Oxford English Dictionary*[2], appeared in October 2009. *OED*, now in the process of revision, has been available as an online resource since 2000, and the *Historical Thesaurus* may be added to it at some point in the future. Dictionaries of current English such as the *Oxford Dictionary of English*[3], the *Collins English Dictionary*[4], and

Merriam-Webster's Collegiate Dictionary[5], are available electronically: as an online resource to which institutions can subscribe, as
data which can be purchased and downloaded, or via CD-ROM.[6]
However, because so many significant reference works have already moved online, we should not assume that there are not
major resources for which print is still the medium.

One of the most notable is the six-volume *English Dialect
Dictionary*, edited by the philologist Joseph Wright (1855–
1930)[7], which appeared in 1905. The first great undertaking for
recording and defining the different varieties of regional English, this monumental work was based on evidence collected
by members of the English Dialect Society over more than
thirty years. When it appeared, the Yorkshire Dialect Society
commented that it was 'undoubtedly the final English Dialect
Dictionary, as the materials from which it is composed are fast
disappearing'. While announcements that no further dictionary of a particular kind can appear are likely to be premature[8],
the Society was right to be aware that the world of closed rural
communities, many members of which would not travel
beyond their own borders, was coming to an end. What they
did not foresee was that in the unstoppable process of language change, many of the dialects identified would change
and adapt, be affected by the outside world, but still retain a
recognizable identity.

Another major work, now nearing completion, is the *Dictionary of American Regional English* (*DARE*), the first volume of
which (A–C) was published in 1985. To date *DARE* comprises
four volumes, with the most recent, P–Sk, having appeared in
2002, and with the final volume due in 2011. The *DARE* website carries a statement of use which makes it clear that the

essential value of a resource does not depend upon its being electronically available, although such availability certainly maximizes use. Specialist users of the dictionary include teachers, writers, forensic linguists, doctors (who use it to understand folk medical terms employed by their patients), scientists (who use it to identify plants and animals called by their local folk names), and oral historians working on the documentation of earlier periods. *DARE* is also used by general readers for pleasure in the quotations that illustrate every entry.

The *DARE* website (www.dare.wisc.edu) illustrates another point: the degree to which use of a complex print resource can be made easier and more fruitful by the provision of a website with background information (such as a history of the project), and sample entries including one in which key elements of the structure are highlighted and explained. A list of Frequently Asked Questions (FAQs), and their answers, may well resolve the question which has brought the reader to the website.[9] There is a full index of all terms used in the entry labels in the published volumes, so that under K it is possible to find references to all the terms labelled as used in Kansas or Kentucky. The section on 'Educational Resources' includes *DARE* audio samples, and a video of a lecture on the dictionary by the Chief Editor. To have access to these supplementary resources while exploring the riches of the printed volumes undoubtedly helps the reader to take best advantage of a complex and fascinating treasury of language.

Moving online

Plans for *DARE* include a future electronic edition, and increasingly and inevitably large reference projects are moving or

WHO USES *DARE*?

Teachers use *DARE* to help their students understand that EVERYONE speaks a dialect.

Writers use *DARE* to verify the accuracy of their dialogue.

Forensic linguists and detectives use *DARE* to help apprehend and convict criminals.

Physicians use *DARE* to understand the folk medical terms used by their patients.

Natural scientists use *DARE* to equate local folk names for plants and animals with the corresponding scientific names.

Librarians use *DARE* to answer queries from their patrons.

Actors and dialect coaches use *DARE*'s audiotape collection to perfect their regional accents.

Oral historians use *DARE* to document the experiences of our ancestors.

And DARE is used by readers who simply delight in the variety, wit, and wisdom found in the quotations that illustrate each entry in the Dictionary.

'Who uses *DARE*?' panel from website of the *Dictionary of American Regional English* website.

have already moved online. The revised edition of the *Oxford English Dictionary*, currently in progress, is being published electronically with quarterly updates appearing online; print volumes seem increasingly to be a thing of the past. The *Dictionary of the Scots Language* (*DSL*, www.dsl.ac.uk), available since 2004, comprises electronic editions of two earlier historical dictionaries, the *Dictionary of the Older Scottish Tongue* (*DOST*) and the *Scottish National Dictionary* (*SND*). The 'enquiring reader' can search across both texts together or only one of them, and ancillary material provided includes language maps of Scotland, and a 'History of Scots to 1700'.

The last part of the *Scottish National Dictionary* was published in 1976, but as the background information provided by the website points out, 'Scots is a living language'. New words and senses are likely to appear as part of the process of language change. More recent material is still being compiled, and the intention is to add to what is already available on the *DSL* website, 'to bring the lexicographic record of Scots truly up to date'.

DSL envisages adding new material to the existing record, but since March 2008 the updates to the *Oxford English Dictionary* have demonstrated another key virtue of online publication: the ability to revise text across the whole alphabetic sequence. The Chief Editor, John Simpson, explained the importance of this change in an accompanying piece (http://dictionary.oed.com/news/updates/revisions0803.html), and it is worth considering the salient points. The main purpose, clearly stated, was to 'revise, much earlier than would otherwise have been the case, important English words whose meanings or application have developed most over the past century'. The systematic alphabetic editing was at that time in M. The new policy made possible revision of such key terms as *aeroplane* (the unrevised entry dated from 1884), *airwave*, *cancer*, *computer*, *electronic, evolution, gay,* and *gene,* which previously had presented definitions from a period prior to significant scientific development and social change.

Apart from the obvious value when a dictionary text of some antiquity is being revised for today's reader, this raises another point. Language changes swiftly: new words are added, or uses from the past may gain extra significance in the light of current events. A dictionary which is edited and revised online is likely to be regularly updated: a text which has been captured for CD-ROM[10] remains fixed in its original form. However, this may not mean that there is no associated material which does reflect what is happening in the more recent language. Thus, while the CD-ROM of the eleventh edition of *Merriam-Webster's Collegiate Dictionary* offers definitions which were published in 2003, the associated online newsletter *Word.com* regularly provides information about the language of the day. The issue for January 2010 included a short history of the word *avatar*—which in December, following the release of James Cameron's blockbuster film, had been number one of Merriam-Webster's top twenty list of most-looked-up words for the month.

There are of course language resources which were created as online sites. These may vary in speciality and type. Paul McFedries's *Word Spy: the Word Lover's Guide to New Words* (www.wordspy.com) and Michael Quinion's *World Wide Words* (www.worldwidewords.org) offer a mediated approach in which the site editor defines, annotates, and comments. Wordnik (www.wordnik.com), launched in 2009, combines information about words, links to existing dictionaries, and sample sentences with postings from contributors. The focus of the

avatar

A word may begin its life in a language with a very specific meaning and area of use, and then move into wider use. *Avatar*, which entered English in the late eighteenth century (and which comes ultimately from Sanskrit), originally denoted a term in Hinduism for the incarnation of a divine being on earth in human form. In a few decades, it was being used more generally for the embodiment of a person or an idea. Then, in the late twentieth century, *avatar* took on a new life in another specific region, as a term in computer games and science fiction for a person or character in a computer-generated environment. Most recently, in late 2009, the release of James Cameron's blockbuster film *Avatar* triggered intense public interest in the word: to the point that the dictionary publishers Merriam-Webster listed it as the most-looked-up word on their website for December 2009.

user-generated *Urban Dictionary* (www.urbandictionary.com), set up in 1999, is on slang words and phrases. Contributors post their own selected words and phrases, definitions, and examples. Since all dictionaries and websites will have their own criteria, it can often be rewarding to try a word or phrase across a range of resources, in print or online.

Corpus delicti

The websites considered above all offer in some form the function of a dictionary: they allow us to look up a word to find out what it means and (perhaps) where it comes from.

However, there is another type of language resource which it is appropriate to consider here. One of the gifts of the electronic age to language research is the development of the language corpus, which allows very large sets of data to be searched for words and phrases, and which returns the results showing the use in context. Major dictionary houses are likely to have their own resources (Oxford dictionaries have built their own Oxford Corpus), but there are sites which are available to the general public. The earliest of these, the British National Corpus (BNC, http://www.natcorp.ox.ac.uk/corpus), compiled between 1991 and 1994, consists of a million words of the spoken and written language. The more recent Corpus of Contemporary American English (COCA, http://www.americancorpus.org), released in 2008, contains over four hundred million words of text, and also represents the spoken and written language. Very importantly, it is updated twice-yearly.

As a resource, a corpus can function as one step back from a dictionary. It will not offer a definition or explicit information about a word, but it can tell us whether it is in use, and let us see how in fact it is being used. A search for a particular word will present the evidence in what is known as KWIC ('key word in context') form, with the word we are seeking shown in the middle of the surrounding words of the passage. Because we are able to see a range of examples, we can often get a sense of how the word is most likely to be used. It may appear predominantly in company with another word or type of word, or as part of a phrase. Alternatively, is it commonly used in a negative or a positive way? And is the example which we have typical, or unusual?

Corpus evidence can provide essential clues in our exploration of an unfamiliar term, and allow us to assess for ourselves how a more familiar term is likely to be used today.

Looking further

The corpora discussed above have been compiled and organized as tools for examining the language. However, while we benefit enormously from the planning that has gone into them, and from their structure (for example, in being able to search across a range of sources and get back a list of lines with our key term in context), it does not mean that we cannot make similar use of other sets of data. Of these, newspaper archives are particularly productive, since they carry a wide range of material, and even (in reporting direct speech) have something of the value of the spoken word.

Some such archives are obtainable as subscription services (and it is always worth checking out your local library facilities to see whether your reader's ticket entitles you to use a resource, as part of a reference package to which the library subscribes). Google News Archive, however, is free, and has features which can maximize the results you get. 'Advanced search' allows you to limit your search between specific days or years. As well as this, on getting your results, you can click on 'Timeline'. The diagram provided not only blocks out the periods at which the word was used, it also shows spikes for times of heavy usage, when the word or phrase in question was associated with (or itself became) a hot topic.

The word *snollygoster* provides an example of this. In the nineteenth century, *snollygoster* was a colourful American term for an unprincipled politician. (Its origin is obscure, but it has been suggested that it is related to the later *snallygaster*, a name in Maryland for a mythical monster, a blend of reptile and bird, deriving ultimately from the German *schnelle Geister*, 'quick spirits'.) *Snollygoster* had appeared rather to fall from sight, and in fact had been dropped by the eleventh edition of *Merriam-Webster's Collegiate Dictionary* in 2003. However, it surfaced in Britain in the early summer of 2009, as part of the debate over MPs' expenses. A candidate for one constituency demanded that the sitting MP should make public all his expenses so that the electorate could be assured that he was not a 'snollygoster'. Investigation of its previous usage history shows that it 'spiked' notably in 1952 and 1953, following US President Harry Truman's reference to 'Republican snollygosters'. The Google News Archive histogram for *snollygoster* immediately draws attention to the pattern of usage.

Other valuable resources may bring together a wide range of texts from a particular period. The primary purpose may not be linguistic, but the availability of such material for online searching is extremely valuable. Thus, someone interested in American English of the nineteenth century could turn to the *Making of America* website, an electronic resource compiled as a collection of primary sources in American social history. More widely, resources for genealogical research may lead to valuable information on occupational terms which are no longer current. Dictionaries of national biography may provide leads through descriptions of the activities of a particular person. General encyclopedias, from the *Encyclopaedia Britannica* to *Wikipedia*, may offer a reference or an association which will allow us to take another vital step in our particular search.

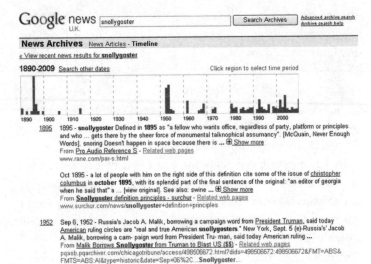

Google News Archive search for *snollygoster* with timeline, showing usage spike in 1952 and 1953.

Finally, of course, we have search engines with functions allowing us to use them as dictionaries: Google, for example, has a 'define' function, in which 'define' is put into the search field preceding the word whose meaning we want to find. A telling phrase in a *Times* column of February 2010 might suggest an alternative to the expression 'look it up in a dictionary'.

encyclopedia

An *encyclopedia* has been a familiar sight on our bookshelves for centuries, but the word has only been part of the language since the sixteenth century. It comes (through late Latin) from a Greek expression *enkuklios paideia* 'all-round education', that is, the arts and sciences considered to be essential to a liberal education. Sir Thomas Elyot's *The Boke named The Gouernour* (1531) uses it: 'The circle of doctrine . . . is in one worde of greke Encyclopedia.' In the following century, the word was naturally extended to mean a literary work which provided extensive information on many subjects, or on many aspects of one subject, typically arranged in alphabetical order.

The origin of the word is helpful in reminding us of the essential difference between an encyclopedia and a dictionary. An encyclopedia gives us information about a subject, while a dictionary lists and defines words. There is, inevitably, a degree of overlap, but the distinction is worth remembering when considering to which possible source we should turn. There may also be interest in a further reflection. Referring to someone as a *walking encyclopedia* is likely to be positive: as the American lawyer and politician William Wirt wrote of Thomas Jefferson in 1833, 'Mr Jefferson was, himself, a living and walking encyclopedia.' The expression contrasts with the criticism of someone given to using long words and over-formal phrasing, that they have *swallowed a dictionary*.

The columnist referred to 'those of us who need to google the word algorithm to check what it means'—a usage which suggests how natural the process has become.

Ways of saying it

Dictionaries and corpora both function on the assumption that we wish to investigate the identity and nature of a particular word: typically either to discover its meaning or history, or to gain a better understanding of exactly how it is used. There is however another major category of language resource to consider: the thesaurus. As we saw briefly in the first chapter[11], while dictionaries are organized on the assumption that what the reader wants to do is to look up the meaning and origin of a particular word, the purpose of the thesaurus is to identify key concepts to which groups of words belong. We can look up a topic or concept, and find a range of words which fall within its range. And as with lexical dictionaries, when we look more closely, we find a wide range of publications available.

The first thesaurus (as noted in the panel on p. 69) was Roget's in 1852, and the book is still (in its one hundred and fiftieth anniversary edition) with us. It is now, understandably, only one of a number of such collections, including (as noted above) the magisterial *Historical Thesaurus of the Oxford English Dictionary*, which allows us to trace synonyms and related terms for things and concepts through the centuries.

Always something new

Proverbial wisdom tells us that there is 'always something new out of Africa'; we could add that there will always be something new in the area of language resource, especially as modern technology enables major projects to tap into many sources of the spoken and written language. Despite the

thesaurus

In February 2010, the *Guardian* newspaper asked a number of writers for their 'golden rules' for writing. The Canadian author Margaret Atwood included the practical advice that the aspiring writer should have a thesaurus (along with 'a rudimentary grammar book, and a grip on reality'). A thesaurus as a tool for finding exactly the right word is seen as so essential that it is worth pausing to see how long the name for this type of resource has been with us. Exploration of the background takes us down a bypath of reference history.

Thesaurus, coming through Latin from the Greek word *thēsauros* 'storehouse, treasure', has been found in English from the late sixteenth century, and originally meant 'dictionary or encyclopedia'. However, in 1852 the physician and philologist Peter Mark Roget published his seminal *Thesaurus of English Words and Phrases, classified and arranged so as to facilitate the expression of ideas, and assist in literary composition*. It was an immediate and lasting success (the *Oxford Dictionary of National Biography* entry for Roget notes that it has gone through many editions and has never been out of print), and it achieved for its author what was probably the unintended distinction of creating not just a new sense of the word, but one which became the only sense in which *thesaurus* is now used. (A particularly notable reference from the early twentieth century is found in Barrie's *Peter Pan*, in which it constitutes an argument on behalf of Captain Hook: 'The man is not wholly evil: he has a Thesaurus in his cabin.')

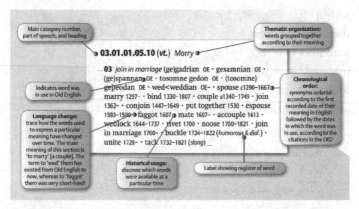

Exploded entry from the *Historical Thesaurus of the Oxford English Dictionary*, showing verbs meaning 'to marry'.

gloomy predictions of the Yorkshire Dialect Society at the beginning of the twentieth century, some of the healthiest relate to studies of regional English in today's world.

One was the BBC 'Voices' Project, launched in the first decade of the twenty-first century. Spearheaded by language experts at the University of Leeds, the project's aim was to record and evaluate attitudes to regional variation of the spoken word across the United Kingdom. The voices of at least one thousand interviewees were to be recorded, and contributors were encouraged to make known their points of view by taking part in an online survey.

The project was publicly launched in January 2005, and the response was enthusiastic, resulting in a treasury of information (an account of the material, plus valuable links to related sources, is to be found at the BBC website for the project, http://www.bbc.co.uk/voices). Linguists at the University of Leeds are currently working on the data, and their own website has something interesting to say on the response from the public. A press release of 25 May 2007 announced that researchers had received a grant to examine and catalogue the material. It pointed out that 'perhaps the most remarkable finding' in the Voices study was that despite increased mobility and exposure to television and radio, the English language was 'as diverse as ever'. The press release continued:

> It reveals an amazing range of words to describe the simplest things. While a Yorkshire youngster would wear his pumps to meet his mate in the snicket, his Scots counterpart might wear gutties to see his pal in the close, while on the south coast he could wear his daps to meet a butty in the twitten.
>
> —'Mapping the English language—from cockney to Orkney', press release, University of Leeds, 25 May 2007 (http://reporter.leeds.ac.uk/press_releases/current/voices.htm)

When the findings were made available online by the BBC, they 'provoked a huge response—with more than a million hits on the website and thousands of on-line posts'. This was clearly testimony both to the widespread interest and pride in varieties of English, and to the durability of diversity. Hearteningly, the forecast of the Yorkshire Dialect Society in 1905 referred to above now seems less prescient.

More recently, another major language enterprise was highlighted in news stories of January 2010, announcing the establishment of the 'Australian Voices' website. A headline in the *Sydney Morning Herald* of 25 January 2010, 'It's all English, but vowels ain't voils', introduced an account of the project, based at Macquarie University, to study Australian English. A key part of the programme will be to invite Australians to submit recordings of their speech, and the website already provides riches of written and recorded material for someone wanting to explore the range of Australian English.

The lesson is that we can never be sure that our list of resources is complete. There may always be another project to amass data and explore a region of the language.

Chapter 5

The Art of Exploration (ii): how to look for answers

WHILE some questions can be resolved immediately by recourse to a dictionary, each dictionary needs to be approached carefully to ensure that we can make the best use of its riches.

Nobody reads introductions

'Nobody reads introductions' might be described as a publishing truism, however painful to the feelings of an author who has made considerable efforts to explain key facts about their book. In 1915 H. G. Wells published (under a pseudonym) a novel, *Boon*, in which he satirized his fellow writer Henry James. *Boon*, according to the title page, was 'a first selection from the literary remains of George Boon', which had been 'prepared for publication by Reginald Bliss' (enticingly said to be the author of a range of titles from 'The Cousins of Charlotte Brontë' to 'Whales in Captivity'). The book included 'an ambiguous introduction by H. G. Wells', which opened:

> Whenever a publisher gets a book by one author he wants an Introduction written to it by another, and Mr. Fisher Unwin is no exception to the rule. Nobody reads

> Introductions, they serve no useful purpose, and they
> give no pleasure, but they appeal to the business mind, I
> think, because as a rule they cost nothing.
> —'R. Bliss' [H. G. Wells] *Boon* (1915), p. 5

Having commented on 'a certain inseparable intimacy' between Reginald Bliss and himself, he provided a further endorsement:

> I will confess that I have not read his book through,
> though I have a kind of first-hand knowledge of its con-
> tents, and that it seems to me an indiscreet, ill-advised
> book...
> —'R. Bliss' [H. G. Wells] *Boon* (1915), p. 5

Wells's satire works particularly well at this point as he is clearly relying on the reader's recognizing the situation: introductions are likely to go unread.

Towards the end of the twentieth century, the late writer and critic William Safire was similarly unenthusiastic about introductions; he was also ready to put forward an explanation:

> The word introduction spooks me; nobody reads intro-
> ductions. Most readers want to get to the meat of a book
> and scorn the foreword, even when misspelled.
> —William Safire *Adventures in the Word Trade* (1997),
>   p. xiv

With reference books, and especially dictionaries, getting 'to the meat' too hastily may well mean that we have failed to take account of the criteria by which entries have been selected and assembled. We need to be sure that we are approaching the right dictionary for an answer about (for example) a new

Pronunciation Spellings Etymology Quotations Date chart

name, n. and adj.

A. n.

I. A designation.

1. a. A proper noun; a word or phrase constituting the individual designation by which a particular person or thing is known, referred to, or addressed.

Christian, code-, household, maiden, pen-, pet, stage, street name, etc.: see the first element. See also FIRST NAME n., FORENAME n., PLACE NAME n., and SURNAME n.

a **OE** *Death of Edgar* (Parker) 12 Feng his bearn syððan to cynerice, cild unweaxen, eorla ealdor, þam wæs Eadweard nama. **OE** *Bounds* (Sawyer 864) in A. Campbell *Charters of Rochester* (1973) 38 On utwealda Broccesh[a]m ðæs dennes nama, & þæs oðres dennes nama Sængethryc. **OE** *Beowulf* 78 Scop him Heort naman se þe his wordes geweald wide hæfde. **OE** *Beowulf* 343 Beowulf is min nama. **IOE** *Anglo-Saxon Chron.* (Laud) anno 1118, Dises geares eac forðferde se papa Paschalis, & feng Iohan of Gaitan to þam papdome, þam wæs oðer nama Gelasius. **a1225**(?a1200) *MS Trin. Cambr.* in R. Morris *Old Eng. Homilies* (1873) 2nd Ser. 91 Þat mai ech man understonden þe wot wat bitocneð þese tweie names betfage and ierusalem. **c1300** *St. Mary Magdalen* (Laud) 18 in C. Horstmann *Early S.-Eng. Legendary* (1887) 462 In þe Castel of Magdale his faire wumman was i-bore; heo was icleoped in propre name 'þe Maudeleyne' riȝt þare-fore. **c1330**(?a1300) *Sir Tristrem* (1886) l. 1216 Marchaund ich haue ben ay, Mi nam is tramtris. **a1393** GOWER *Confessio Amantis* (Fairf.) II. 947 The kinges Moder there lay, Whos rihte name was Domilde. **a1450**(a1425) J. MIRK *Instr. Parish Priests* (Claud.) 138 Then may the fader..Crysten the chylde and ȝeue hyt name. **c1475** *Mankind* 51 My dame seyde my name was Raffe. **1488**(c1478) HARY *Actis & Deidis Schir William Wallace* (Adv.) l. 321 Schir Malcom Wallas was his nayme. **1531** *Pylgrimage of Perfection* (new ed.) f. 24, Marke therin the citees names & other places in his mynde. **1535** *Bible* (Coverdale) Matt. i. 25 He..called his name Iesus. **1560** L. DAUS tr. J. Sleidane *Commentaries* f. cccvij, A sonne named Henry..the seuenth of that name. **a1616** SHAKESPEARE *Merry Wiues of Windsor* (1623) l. iv. 13 Peter Simple, you say your name is? **1651** T. HOBBES *Leviathan* III. xxxiv. 213 God needeth not, to distinguish his Celestiall servants by names. **1699** in J. Robertson & C. Innes *Munimenta Univ. Glasguensis* (1854) II. 542 A custome of printing the whol nams of the students. **1749** J. CLELAND *Mem. Woman of Pleasure* I. 58, I was too strongly mov'd at the bare mention of his name. **1776** GIBBON *Decline & Fall* I. vi. 156 The name of Antoninus..had been communicated by adoption to the dissolute Verus. **1802** R. SOUTHEY *Life* II. 195 An onymous house too..its name is Maes Gwyn. **1818** SHELLEY *Julian & Maddalo* 584 The name Of Venice, and its aspect, was the same. **1897** *Cent. Mag.* July 257 He would call them sometimes by their last names. **1909** L. M. MONTGOMERY *Anne of Avonlea* xx. 234 Mrs. Morgan wanted to know how the Haunted Wood came by its name. **1953** S. CHASE *Power of Words* i. vii. 79 His name is Usak, a seal hunter of the Netsilik tribe of Eskimos. **2000** *Esquire* Dec. 110/1 If you're going to keep staring at me, you might as well know my name.

Revised *Oxford English Dictionary* entry for *name*, showing first sense and quotation block.

word, a slang term, a dialect expression, or a meaning which was current at an earlier period.

If we take it that there is a general probability in print volumes that the reader will 'skip over the introduction'[1], it seems highly likely that the propensity would extend to background information provided by websites. This would again be a serious mistake, since it is crucial to understand exactly what it is that we are seeing.

When we consult a print volume, it is not difficult to know whether or not we have an up-to-date text. Multi-volume dictionaries of the late nineteenth and early twentieth centuries were large and handsome volumes, often with leather binding, good-quality paper, and clear traditional fonts. Publication history was recorded on the reverse of the title page of each volume. However, when a text is made available online, it may be much less apparent whether or not the content originates in the present day, or from a much earlier period. It is therefore important both to be alert to implicit evidence (for example, if an entry includes illustrative examples, noting what date range is covered), and even more to read any background information provided.

Word searching: traditional and online

Whether we are turning the pages of a nineteenth-century reference resource, or conducting online searches through a website of today, some techniques are the same. In each case, we need to formulate our questions clearly, and be alert to any clues which the text we are looking at may give us. The key differences lie in the types of systematic searches that we can pursue.

In December 2009, the website for www.laterooms.com had an article on the Nice Christmas Fair, which offered 'Provençal specialities such as honey, lavender and traditional Santons'. In the late 1970s, researching possible entries for the ongoing *Supplement to the Oxford English Dictionary*, I was given the word *santon*[2]—a name for small pottery figures in a Nativity scene, which the modern quotations we had to hand indicated were typical of Provence. We had evidence of use from the late twentieth century: we needed to find earlier examples of the word in English.

The nature of the word provided obvious starting points. It was a borrowing from French, and it was associated with a particular region. That meant it was possible to identify an immediate area for research: travel accounts of the area. Books of this kind, especially as written in the late nineteenth and early twentieth centuries, are often characterized by a chatty style and references to local customs. It was therefore worth the expenditure of time involved in finding the relevant section in the library stack, and scanning pages and indexes (if the book in question had an index) for key expressions like 'Christmas' and 'feast', as well as for the word itself. (It was of course also helpful that, as a borrowing, the word in earlier use was likely to be printed in italics: always a guide to the eye.) The search was rewarded: *A Wayfarer in Provence* by E. I. Robson provided a 1926 example of the word in context in a reference to: 'the little home-made crèches, the simple figures known as the Santons'.

Scanning printed texts by eye to find a single word is inevitably time-consuming, and 1926 was quite a 'good' date. It took the word back to the first half of the twentieth century, into the period following the First World War when there was once again time, leisure, and money to explore corners of Europe, and write about them for an audience at home.

As a library researcher to the *Supplement to the Oxford English Dictionary*, I had the good fortune (and great privilege) to have special access to the stacks (restricted areas) of a major research library (the Bodleian), in which books had been classified, and then shelved chronologically. I was able therefore to find the appropriate section for travel writing, and browse along the shelves in the underground book stack. What I did not have, of course, were the online resources which today a researcher would take for granted.

At the time in which I was working, none of the major library catalogues was electronically available: there was no possibility of searching online for likely sources, and existing print catalogues were organized according to author and title rather than subject. Still less was it possible to search across the full text of a great number of digitized books from earlier decades and centuries. In April 2010 (when this book went to press), the revised entry for *santon* had not been published by the *Oxford English Dictionary*, so Robson's use stood as the earliest example of this sense of the word. However, even a quick online search reveals that it was likely to be antedated: an issue of the *Atlantic Monthly* of 1908 carried a reference to 'an artist of the Santons or Santouns—the clay images made in thousands for the Christmas *crèches*'.

With traditional methods of word searching, time is inevitably spent in finding and handling physical volumes, and then in scanning by eye. Online results are achieved more quickly, but this has its own drawbacks. It is possible (often likely) that rather than failing to find anything, we will receive a flood of returns, all of which then have to be filtered.

Santon is a case in point, not least because the meaning in which we are interested is only one sense of the word. Before embarking on an online search, it is essential to be aware of what the possible results are. Checking in a dictionary which covers the historical language reveals that originally (from the sixteenth century) the term *santon* was applied by Western travellers to holy men seen in the east. An online search for the word alone, therefore, is likely to trawl up a number of instances which have nothing to do with the topic of our search. In fact, a search for *santon* with no qualification returns over one thousand hits, which include not only 'santon' meaning a Muslim holy man (as in Edward Bulwer-Lytton's novel *Leila: or, the siege of Granada*, 1865), but also 'Santon' as a place name or personal name.

There are two easy ways of cutting down the number of irrelevant returns. One is to try a search for *santons* in the plural, since it seems likely that the references we want will refer to figurines as a type, rather than to a single model. This alone cuts the number of returns to under seven hundred. If we then add 'Christmas' as a second search term, the number of possibilities is significantly reduced to well under two hundred.[3]

'This rotten book'

In one of Montague Rhodes James's short stories, 'The Mezzotint', published in *Ghost Stories of an Antiquary* (1904), we are given a vivid picture of the frustration of a researcher following traditional methods, who has not entirely matched expectation to resource.

In this story, it is a matter of some anxiety to identify a building reproduced in the mezzotint of the title. The only clues are given by a torn label with 'the ends of two lines of writing: the first had the letters –*ngley Hall*; the second, –*ssex*'. The conclusion is that the name must have been 'Somethingley Hall, either in Sussex or Essex'. When a fellow scholar can give no help, the only option is recourse to a gazetteer:

> Williams was engaged in a vain attempt to identify the subject of his picture. 'If the vowel before the *ng* had only been left it would have been easy enough,' he thought; 'but as it is, the name may be anything from Guestingley to Langley; and there are many more names ending like this than I had thought; and this rotten book has no index of terminations.
>
> —M. R. James *Ghost Stories of An Antiquary* (1904), 'The Mezzotint'

While sympathizing with the frustration that led Mr Williams to criticize his gazetteer, we must in fairness question whether he could reasonably have expected to find a book which would offer a direct route to the partial name on his torn caption. It is really not surprising that he and his friends, as the urgency of identifying the house increased, decided that 'There was nothing for it but to spend the evening over gazetteers and guide-books.'

It is pleasing to note that in this case, Williams himself was rewarded by finding an entry for 'Anningley Hall' in an Essex guide-book, and the unfolding of the story made it clear that the time he and his friends were prepared to spend on the search was justified. The question, however, is one that we may need to ask ourselves: to what degree continued systematic searching is justified, or whether we have reached the point at which further research is likely to be inordinately time-consuming, and fruitful only through luck.

Williams and his colleagues had no choice but to sit turning pages (they had, of course, identified a manageable number of books to search). Our position, however, is different. The searches generated by a particular language story show how we may find ourselves moving between print and online resources.

That Merseyside sound

Early in 2010, an interview published in the online *Goal.com* with the Dutch Liverpool forward Dirk Kuyt, who has been settled in Merseyside for over three years, included a comment on the family's successful adjustment to local culture and language. The footballer revealed that his eldest daughter was now a fluent English speaker. 'In fact, it's not so much English she speaks as Scouse . . . she talks in a genuine local dialect. Scousers talk with some sounds that are similar to Dutch and my daughter is a proper Scouser.'[4]

A natural response to this story is to want to know more about the Scouse variant of English (and perhaps also more widely to consider the whole question of what dialect is). Answering these questions takes us on a journey in which we can usefully explore the kinds of resource available for a search of this kind.

dialect

In March 2010, the heading 'A–Z of old Devon dialect' on a BBC website announced the publication of a number of words from a glossary of traditional north Devon speech sent in by a listener, in order to 'keep the words out there'—an enterprise we can all applaud.

Apart from the interest of the vocabulary itself, the story says something about our understanding of the term *dialect*: we are likely to associate it with a traditional local or regional form of speech, which is now under threat. However, *dialect* has a wider meaning: properly speaking, it is a particular form of language peculiar to a specific region or social group (an eighteenth-century source cited in the *OED* refers to 'Lawyer's Dialect' as being too hard for someone). In the world of computers, *dialect* designates a particular version of a programming language.

If we look at the origins of the word (first recorded in English in the mid sixteenth century), we can see that the original meaning was associated with philosophy, and denoted the art of investigating the truth of opinions. The word goes back ultimately to Greek *dialektos* 'discourse, way of speaking', from *dialegesthai* 'converse with'—and so comes ultimately from the same base as *dialogue*.

No army or navy?

The linguist Max Weinreich (1894–1969) has made famous[5] a kind of reverse definition: 'Language is a dialect with an army and a navy', and this can be an interesting way of considering the question. We may feel that a separate language is distinguished by more than political divides, but the important point is that what we call a dialect does have many or most of the features which we would think of as characterizing a language.

In its coverage of regional varieties of the spoken language within the United Kingdom, the British Library's 'Sounds Familiar' website identifies the key elements which go to make a dialect. They are the distinctive differences of vocabulary, grammar, and pronunciation, which mark out a particular variety of a language (in this case English). However, and this is the key point, speakers of different regional varieties of English are still recognizably speaking the same overall language, and can understand one another—even if some words are unfamiliar, or a familiar word is pronounced differently. The homepage of the 'Sounds Familiar' website allows us to examine both 'lexical' (that is, choice of words) and 'phonological' (how the words are pronounced) variation from around England, Scotland, Wales, and Northern Ireland.

Mousing for Scouse

Online resources have the great advantage of being able not only to describe pronunciations, but to provide recordings, and by mousing over the Word Map provided by the Regional Voices page of the 'Sounds Familiar' website to select a symbol, we can (for example) read and hear the comments of a native Liverpudlian who had gone back to his old school to become a teacher and who felt 'made up' ('it was a great feeling') on entering the staff room, since it was 'hallowed ground when I was a kid—never ever went inside the staff room'.

The story of the Liverpool forward's family, with which this section opened, referred to the sound of 'Scouse' (that is, the variety of English traditionally spoken on Merseyside), and at this point we might feel that we wanted to investigate this particular form of regional English in more detail. Where should we look for information?

Joseph Wright's *English Dialect Dictionary*, as described in the previous chapter, would have been the place to look for evidence about a particular word, but you cannot pull from its six volumes all the words associated with Lancashire or Liverpool. We need a different approach if we want to get an overall picture of 'Scouse'.

Exploring Scouse

A traditional approach would have been to try to identify books which covered the subject, either through library catalogues (looking for books in the right subject area) or through bibliographies: where possible, always be aware that someone else may have done the basic work for you. It would also be good to get a sense of how early *Scouse* as the name for this regional variety of English is likely to be encountered. We might feel that *Scouse* is a relatively informal term, unlikely to have figured in the titles of scholarly collections of the nineteenth century. To validate this, and glean any other relevant items of information, the first place to look is the *Oxford English Dictionary*: is there an entry for *Scouse*, and what can it tell us?

Scouse does appear in the online *OED*, and provides us with several points of interest. Perhaps the first thing to notice (to ensure that we understand the nature of the source we are exploring) is that the entry is labelled as 'Second Edition': that is, it has not yet been revised by the editors of the ongoing third edition, and the most recent material it can contain will be what was published in the relevant volume of the *OED Supplement*, *O–Scz* (1982).

The *OED* entry gives us the expectable historical information for the specific sense of a word first recorded in 1840 as another name for *lobscouse*[6], a dish of stewed meat, vegetables, and ship's biscuit, which used to form part of a sailor's staple fare. The word was borrowed first to designate a person from the great port of Liverpool, and then to denote the variety of English spoken there. The earliest examples provided by *OED* are respectively 1945 and 1963, and the quotations given would have been the earliest uses found by editors at the time, rather than representing the earliest uses that we could hope to find today. When the penultimate volume of the *Supplement* was being researched and written in the late 1970s, there was none of the capacity for online searching of texts that is available today. Editors (and researchers) were dependent on what could be found through systematic searching of indexes and bibliographies, and scanning relevant books by eye, plus (as always) contributions of material picked up by monitoring current publications.

(The first quotation for *Scouse* in the sense of dialect offers a very nice example of the way in which a word which originally has some kind of limitation can quite suddenly reach a wider audience. The quotation in question, which comes from the *Guardian* of June 1963, runs:

> This rock group suddenly made Liverpool fashionable in the entertainment world. After their first two records it

> became necessary for people in the business in London to
> learn a few words of Scouse.
> —*Guardian* 3 June 1963

The existence of the *Guardian* digital archive allows us to follow this up, and confirm the assumption that it was the growing fame of the Beatles which introduced *Scouse* to the awareness of the wider world.)

At this point we have acquired some essential information about the word *Scouse*, but we are still looking for the wider picture of this particular form of English. Searching online for 'Scouse' and 'dialect' may lead us both to other sites which will allow us to hear the spoken language, and to details of written sources in which this particular form of regional English has been examined and discussed. The most fruitful kind of research often derives from using a mix of online and print resources. Electronic searching may identify the title of an out-of-print book which can then be ordered through a library.

Serendipity

Pursuing a lead requires focus, but we can still pause to enjoy it when the line we are pursuing highlights an interesting byway. This happened to me when I was looking at the *OED*'s early evidence for the word *lexicographer* (see panel on p. 23). The first citation (in the bibliographically abbreviated form required by extent considerations) appeared as:

> **1658** Rowland *Moufet's Theat. Ins.* 935 Calepine and other
> Lexicographers of his gang.

corpus

In discussions of dictionary-making today, the terms *corpus* and *corpus lexicography* are now commonplace: we are familiar with the concept of dictionaries being underpinned by an analysis of real language provided by machine-readable collections of written or spoken material. However, as with any term which becomes central, it can be interesting to look back at its earlier history, to see how it reached that particular position.

Corpus, Latin word for 'body', is recorded in Middle English as denoting a human or animal body. (Unsurprisingly, the Latin word is also the base of *corpse* and the archaic *corse*. It also formed a number of phrases, notably the name for the Christian feast of *Corpus Christi*, and the legal expression *corpus delicti*, the facts and circumstances constituting a crime.)

It was in the early eighteenth century that *corpus* developed a further significant shift in meaning, to denote a collection of written texts, especially the entire works of a particular author, or a body of writing on a particular subject. The door was now open for the twentieth-century development which is of such interest to dictionaries today.

The source in question, when expanded to its full form, turned out to refer to a translation by John Rowland of an earlier treatise in Latin. The full title of the translated work was:

> *The Theater of Insects; or, Lesser Living Creatures: as bees, flies, caterpillars, spiders, worms, &c. A most elaborate work: by T. Muffet, Dr. of Physick.*

Translated by John Rowland, it had been appended to Edward Topsell's *The History of Four-Footed Beasts and Serpents*, and published in a single volume in 1658.

It was clear from investigation that versions of Moufet/Muffet's name varied. The *Oxford Dictionary of National Biography* has an entry for Thomas Moffet (1553–1604), a physician and naturalist, and gives both 'Moufet' and 'Muffet' as alternative forms of his name. It was the form 'Muffet' which intrigued me: I wondered, given his work on spiders, if there could be any connection with the well-known nursery rhyme. I was delighted to find that both Iona and Peter Opie's *Oxford Dictionary of Nursery Rhymes* (2nd edn, 1997) and *ODNB* confirmed this: Thomas Moffet had a daughter called Patience, and it has sometimes been suggested that she was the 'Little Miss Muffet' who 'sat on a tuffet' and was frightened by a big spider. It is clear that the identification may come into the area of folk etymology, invented after the fact, given that Thomas Moffet died in 1604, and the earliest record of the nursery rhyme is the early nineteenth century. However, this does not spoil the enjoyment of a colourful link which turned up by chance.

One thing leads to another

The Muffet connection was fun in itself, but it did not stop there. I was intrigued by the cheerfully dismissive reference to 'Calepine and his gang of lexicographers', and decided that I would explore that a little further. The first thing was to find the fuller sentence from which the *OED* citation had been extracted.

When traced to its source, it turned out that it came from a passage on the horsefly. The sentence read:

> Calepine and other Lexicographers of his gang, besides
> some Physicians, and even Pliny himself makes this Fly
> one and the same with the Oxe-fly, so that it is very prob-
> able that they did not so heedfully read Aristotle as they
> might, or did not understand his meaning.
> —Thomas Moffet *The Theater of Insects* (1658), trans.
> John Rowland

Further investigation revealed that 'Calepine' was the Italian lexicographer Ambrogio Calepino (1435–1511), an Italian Augustine friar. He was the editor of a famous Latin dictionary first published in 1502, which went through many editions in the sixteenth century, and briefly gave the English language another word for 'dictionary': *calepin*.

The term was in use in the sixteenth and seventeenth centuries, as in John Evelyn's book on the art of copper engraving, *Sculptura* (1662). Evelyn explained that it was his intention in his text to provide clarification for those likely to encounter technical terms when 'reading such books as treat of the mechanical or more liberal subjects'. His choice of vocabulary was the result of 'much diligent collection' from the works of 'sundry authors'; it was not simply based on taking words from dictionaries: 'It is not to show how diligently we have weeded the calepines and lexicons.' Evelyn's use is *OED*'s last piece of quotation evidence for *calepin*, but the entry as a whole constitutes a small piece of lexical, and lexicographical, history.

The final point of interest for me was Moufet's reference to 'Calepine and other Lexicographers of his gang'. The use of *gang* felt oddly informal, at least given the way in which we would be most likely to use *gang* today, to mean an organized group of criminals. But this was resolved by looking at the *OED* entry for the word. In the seventeenth century *gang* could mean simply 'a company of workmen' (Samuel Pepys in his diary for 1668 has an entry which reads 'Home to dinner, with my gang of clerks').

Miss Muffet and her spider, through an Italian friar and his place in lexicographical history, to the implications of the word *gang*, all constituted a diversion from the original question, which was to look at early evidence for the word *lexicographer* in English. But the opening up of such byways is one of the pleasures of exploring a word.

Chapter 6
Interpreting the Evidence: understanding what we have found

EVIDENCE from searching needs to be interpreted carefully, if we are to make the best of what we have found. It can be tempting to assume that we have found a much earlier use of a particular word than sources show, or that we have identified a completely new word. While both these things can happen, there are also traps for the unwary—even lexicographers have succumbed from time to time.

Ghost words and other dangers

The expression 'ghost word' to denote a word or phrase, included in a dictionary, which has never had real existence has been in use since the late nineteenth century. One famous example of the category appeared in *Webster's Second New International Dictionary*, published in 1934. This included an entry for *dord*, said to be a term in physics and chemistry for 'density'. Unfortunately the entry was based on a misreading: the original note from which it was taken was intended as an addition to the entry for the initial letter D: 'D or d' as a contraction for 'density'.

Dord was removed from *Webster's* by 1940[1], and it is fair to say that its particular dangers were more likely to entrap a lexicographer than an ordinary reader. However, there are other areas in which we may need to take care. A tempting misprint may entice (when I was a library researcher for the *Supplement*, an apparently early reference to a 'posh hotel' in a batch of quotations for checking turned out on investigation to have been an error for 'post hotel').

But I was always told . . .

It is worth pausing here to consider the long-cherished popular explanation for *posh*, that it derives from the initial letters of *port out, starboard home*. This supposedly referred to the cooler, and therefore more comfortable, side of ships travelling between Britain and India in the days of the British Raj. An additional suggestion is that the Peninsular and Oriental Steam Navigation Company stamped tickets for cabins of this kind with the letters P.O.S.H. Regrettably, as has been conclusively demonstrated[2], the explanation does not stand up: there is no evidence for tickets of this kind, and no contemporary references of the kind that would exist if the story were genuine.

The revised *Oxford English Dictionary* now sets out the most likely possible origins. Firstly, the adjective may have developed from earlier nouns: *posh* meaning 'money' or 'a dandy', giving rise to an adjective meaning 'wealthy' or 'smart'. It has also been suggested, although it is thought less probable, that the term might come from the Urdu *safed-pōś* 'dressed in white,

well-dressed', which was also used informally and in a deroga-
tory tone to mean 'affluent'. While both these explanations are
of interest in terms of language development, they lack the life
and colour of the popular 'folk' explanation, and it is under-
standable that this is still cherished. There is also a note in the
etymology about a usage in an early P. G. Wodehouse story:

> That waistcoat ... being quite the most push thing of the
> sort in Cambridge.
> —P. G. Wodehouse *Tales of St Austin's* (1903)

(The etymology, having laid out in some detail the various
unsubstantiated theories for the origin of the word, can only
point out with proper caution that it is unclear whether *push* in
the Wodehouse passage might show an earlier variant of the
word in question.)

OED does at least have the space in which to record the familiar explanation, and note why it is not substantiable: smaller
dictionaries with the constraints of space may often have to
limit an etymology to 'Origin unknown', without going into
details of why a popular explanation is unlikely to be correct.

However, that does not mean that it is not of interest: especially when the apocryphal explanation has become so widely
known. In the case of 'port out, starboard home', awareness of
the phrase may well colour someone's understanding of a bit
of social history of a particular period. The fact that it could be
readily accepted may well tell us something of perceptions of
the time and way of life. In any event, as we have already seen,
there are really no limits to the interest we may have in words.
Why not collect colourful explanations, provided we understand the difference between solid evidence and attractive

'after the fact' stories. (It is a regrettable truth that the more colourful an explanation, the more likely it is to be fiction.)

There is certainly no doubt of the interest people feel in this area. References to 'port out, starboard home' have been with us for half a century, and a column in the *Ottawa Citizen* of May 1959 has a section headed 'Posh Explanation' which opens with the wry comment, 'The word "posh" nearly wrecked a good party a friend gave recently.' The columnist went on to explain that while everyone 'more or less' agreed on the meaning, 'we almost fought over where the word comes from'. Various explanations were put forward, but it was only after the party that the columnist was given what he thought was 'a perfect explanation'. It was, perhaps inevitably, that the letters stood for 'Port Out, Starboard Home', from the days when 'wealthy Britishers were booking ship passage to visit their vast holdings in India'. The column, while not necessarily adding to etymological clarification, has a real interest in terms of social history. And the story of the dinner party reminds us of how strongly people feel about their entrenched beliefs.

Does it really mean that?

A word may appear in a context which suggests that a real shift of sense has taken place—but can we be absolutely certain that there is no ambiguity? To get a feeling for how easy it can be to misinterpret through context, it is helpful to look at the revised *Oxford English Dictionary* entry for the adjective *gay*, in what is now the dominant modern sense of 'homosexual'. While the entry makes clear that the first unquestionable use of the term comes from American English in 1941, the dictionary also provides a sample of earlier quotations (going back to 1922) which have been suggested as early uses in this sense. The accompanying note points out that while there may well have been conscious innuendo in some cases, it is likely that current understanding of context (including an author's sexuality) have led to an anachronistic interpretation.

The point is quite nicely made by the fact that two of the quotations come from lyrics by Noël Coward, for example: 'Everyone's here and frightfully gay', which continues with a reference to the Riviera seeming 'really much queerer Than Rome at its height'.[3]

Coward's own inner circle might well have recognized and been amused by the double meaning, but Coward himself was keenly aware of what was and was not at that time likely to be consonant with his image with the theatre-going public. His biographer Sheridan Morley recalled Coward's refusal to be 'outed' despite the example of the theatre critic T. C. Worsley. In his life of Coward, *A Talent to Amuse*, published in 1986, Morley recalled Coward's crushing and final rejoinder on the topic: 'The British public at large would not care if Cuthbert Worsley had slept with mice.'

We cannot, in strict lexicographical terms, accept the quotations as definite evidence for the use of the word in this sense, but (as the *OED* treatment recognizes) we can find them of distinct interest in the history of the word. And this, of course, is one of the advantages a word enthusiast may have over a lexicographer. *OED* is a large enough dictionary (especially now that the text is edited and published online) to provide this kind of background information for key words. But even for electronic texts, space is not unlimited: often a lexicographer is limited to providing the conclusions they have reached, rather than offering some of the fascinating background stories with which they have dealt. Those of us who are not compiling a dictionary can be less strict: we can allow ourselves to collect and enjoy relevant material. To be aware that a particular instance does not present an unquestionable illustration of a new sense does not mean that it may not be of interest in the light of later developments. The key point, though, is that we should understand exactly what it is that we have found.

Risky assumptions

Some of the traps we may fall into are signalled by the existence of special terms: for example, *false friends*. A 'false friend' is a word or expression which has a close resemblance to one in another language, and which may therefore be taken as having the same meaning. Thus, while French *magasin* 'shop' resembles English *magazine*, the primary sense of the English word has now developed to mean a journal or paper. German *Gift* means 'poison' rather than 'a present'. English *cold* and German *kalt* both have the same meaning; in Italian and Spanish, however, *caldo* means 'hot'. Anyone who has visited a Roman villa, and seen the site of the *caldarium*, can probably remember initial confusion as to whether this offered a hot (which in fact it did) or a cold bath. False friends are particularly dangerous if we are trying to work out a meaning from perhaps scanty knowledge of the foreign language from which a borrowing has come.

Similar dangers may lurk in the existence of homonyms: words which are spelt exactly the same, but which have a completely different origin and meaning. To take one example, a column in the *Omaha World-Herald* of 13 February 2010 requested readers to send in holiday memories, in anticipation of a forthcoming exhibition to be entitled 'Are We There Yet?' The opening sentence reads: 'Memories of family vacations often involve a memorable vehicle: a "family truckster", a cramped sedan or a roomy van.' (The inverted commas round 'family truckster' suggest that there is something unusual about the phrase, and this may be reinforced by the tendency of a spellchecker to correct the word to 'trickster'.)

As always, our first recourse is to a dictionary, but in this case it is less than helpful: either (in the case of dictionaries of the current language) it does not appear, or it turns up with what looks like a completely different meaning. The *Shorter Oxford English Dictionary* has an entry for *truckster* (labelled as a rare word, dating from the mid nineteenth century) in which it is defined as a pedlar or huckster. The origin is from the verb *truck* meaning barter or bargain. There is no connection with *truck* in the sense of a wheeled vehicle.

At this point, we need to look for other ways of getting to our objective. In this case, the obvious thing is to go back to gathering primary evidence. The Corpus of Contemporary American English (COCA) offers four examples of the word, all of which give it in the compound 'family truckster'. All make it clear that what is being discussed is a vehicle, as in (from a 2000 report on CNN) 'Some say the four-wheel-drive gas guzzlers have become the indispensable family truckster.' It looks, therefore, as though 'family truckster' might be a productive search term. If we use it in Google News Archive we get a number of references, with a particularly promising headline from the *Tahoe Daily Tribune* of June 2005, 'The family truckster is no longer fashionable for modern Griswolds.' With this extra clue, and the News Archive timeline showing hits back to 1983, it is not difficult to get to the source: Chevy Chase's 1983 film *National Lampoon's Vacation*. The family in the story, setting out on a two-week drive to a famous amusement park, do so in an enormous and inconvenient 'Wagon Queen Family Truckster', which 'Clark W. Griswold' (Chevy Chase) has unwisely been persuaded to buy.

The *truckster*, therefore, was originally a humorous coinage: a name for a vehicle which was a parody of what any sensible family would want. It looks, however, as though in the phrase 'family truckster' it may have won itself a place in the language.

At this point, we could leave the matter, but to get the full picture it is worth doing a further archive search for *truckster* alone. Interestingly, this turns up a number of (North American) uses from the 1920s onward, in which the word is used either to denote a type of haulage vehicle, or as another word for *trucker*. This gives us a fuller picture: the word (with the meaning of someone or something associated with the truck as a vehicle) has existed at least since the early twentieth century, but it was the 1983 film which propelled it into a different level of familiarity and usage.

The historical *truckster*, on the other hand, may have fallen by the wayside. The most recent citation in the *OED* is from a 1931 source, Alison Uttley's *A Country Child*, in which she recalls a pedlar with 'a pack on his back containing . . . all the odds and ends of the truckster'. Perhaps part of the reason for this contrast is that, while etymologically both words are formed by adding the suffix –*ster* (denoting a person or thing engaged in or associated with a particular activity), one derives from an extremely familiar word (*truck* as a vehicle), and one from a word which is now uncommon (*truck* meaning to barter or bargain).

I'm sure I remember . . .

Sometimes we can be puzzled by what we do *not* find: an earlier record of a word or phrase which we are sure we remember from our childhood, or an apparent recollection of the words we believe someone to have used. At times, the failure may simply mean that we have come to a dead end in our search, but at other times our memory may be at fault. We often edit as we repeat, paraphrasing and condensing an original sentence or passage. Unintentionally, the words we retain carry the gist of the meaning, but may well not be an exact match for what we originally heard or read. Interpreting the results when we do reach a dead end can suggest whether or not there should be a further step, even if frustratingly we are not at that point able to take it.

Oliver's advice

Years ago I had personal experience of this, when researching the phrase *keep one's powder dry* for the *Supplement to the Oxford English Dictionary*. The expression comes directly from the proverbial saying, *Put your trust in God, and keep your powder dry*, and is traditionally said to represent Oliver Cromwell's advice to troops when fording a river. The earliest source in which it appears is a poem, 'Oliver's Advice', first published in 1834, and included (attributed to 'Colonel Blacker') in the 1856 collection *Ballads of Ireland*. Each verse of the poem concluded with the salient words, as in the ominous opening lines:

> The night is gathering gloomily, the day is closing fast—
> The tempest flaps his raven wings in loud and angry blast—
> The thunder clouds are driving athwart the lurid sky—
> Then put your trust in God, my boys, and keep your powder dry.
> —Colonel Blacker 'Oliver's Advice' in E. Hayes (ed.)
> *Ballads of Ireland* (1856)

Other verses, with references to William III, the Battle of the Boyne, and the Irish Insurrection of 1798, are fully in tune with a Protestant Ascendancy view of Irish history, and the use of the key phrase is explained in a footnote which claims that:

> There is a well-authenticated anecdote of Cromwell. On a certain occasion, when his troops were about crossing a river to attack the enemy, he concluded an address, couched in the usual fanatic terms in use among them, with these words: 'Put your trust in God: but mind to keep your powder dry.
> —footnote to Colonel Blacker 'Oliver's Advice' in E. Hayes (ed.) *Ballads of Ireland* (1856)

The explicit mention of a 'well-authenticated anecdote' is backed up by implicit evidence. The actual name 'Cromwell' does not appear anywhere in the poem. It was clearly expected that anyone hearing the poem, with its title 'Oliver's Advice', would understand the reference. It should therefore have been possible to take one further step, and trace the original story: not necessarily to a contemporary source, but at least to a later publication, prior to the mid nineteenth century, which recorded apocryphal and other anecdotes. However, I was not able to find this either in earlier publications, or by looking at modern sources for a reference. I had to leave things as they stood, while believing (in some frustration) that by 1834 the story of Cromwell using the expression 'Put your trust in God, and keep your powder dry' was already known, and that a written record did exist somewhere.

Enter Rumour

At times, of course, we are quite right to be suspicious, as can be demonstrated by a news story of February 2010. The scientist Sir John Houghton had issued a statement, protesting about a 'quotation' (in relation to climate change) regularly attributed to him, 'Unless we announce disasters, no one will listen.' A number of references give as a specific source a book on global warming which he published in 1994, although in fact the words do not appear there. As he pointed out in an interview with the British newspaper the *Independent*:

> There are those who will say 'unless we announce disasters, no one will listen,' but I'm not one of them. It's not the sort of thing I would ever say. It's quite the opposite of what I think, and it pains me to see this quote being used repeatedly in this way.
> —Sir John Houghton, interview in *Independent*, 10 February 2010

As the *Independent* coverage noted, the quotation (so-called) currently appeared on about one hundred and thirty thousand web pages. In this case, the resulting publicity did demonstrate that the attribution was indeed apocryphal, but the story does have a wider application. If we come across a widely-cited quotation apparently from a specific source, it is desirable to track down the original and see whether the words are actually there, and in that form.

If we find references to a named source but no direct quotation (either giving a wider context for the words in question, or a precise page reference), we may wonder how solid it is. It is also worth, if we have a year date, seeing how far back citations occur in (for example) news sources. In this instance, the originating source was supposed to be from 1994. However, a search on Google News Archive for the string 'unless we announce disasters' turns up 2006 as the earliest appearance of the quotation. The twelve-year gap again prompts the desirability of checking how valid the reference to the earlier date is likely to be.

Electronic resources do have their downside. The second part of Shakespeare's *Henry IV* begins with the stage direction, 'Enter Rumour, painted full of tongues', and that could be taken as an image of what can happen on the internet.[4] Words and phrases are passed round and commented on, and it does not take long for something to establish an impressive presence: searches for the item will return a considerable number of hits. It is quite likely, also, that an initial speculation about meaning or origin will be repeated as solid fact. We therefore need, when looking at online results, to be properly sceptical, and to be alert to danger signs. Fortunately, as the foregoing example shows, the medium which disseminates a word or (supposed) saying also offers us the chance to track it, and to assess the balance of evidence for it.

Solid ground

At this point, it may be a relief to return to solid material, and look at what reliable quotations may tell us, beyond the fact that a particular word or phrase was in use at a certain period. On some occasions, it is possible to draw cautious conclusions about social history from linguistic evidence.

In the 1980s, vocabulary reflecting food from around the world was increasingly a commonplace, and many of these terms were collected for the *Supplement to the Oxford English Dictionary*. This meant that we needed to look for earlier usage examples. In those days, we had no online searching, so what was required was to identify books which might use names for foreign dishes. The two main categories were travel writing (where the traveller might have encountered a particular form of food, and been helpful enough to give its name rather than simply saying what it was like) and cookery books. The latter group showed an interesting pattern.

Today, we are used to libraries and bookshops carrying a wealth of titles featuring dishes of the world; we are likely to be able to buy the ingredients from which to make them. Beyond this, recipes from around the world can be found on the internet. There is no real sense that information about food from a particular region might be out of reach. However, in Britain before the Second World War, it was a very different matter. Cookery books focused on traditional European

vocabulary

Today when we come across the word *vocabulary* it is likely to be in the sense of the body of words making up a particular language, or the range of language known or used in a particular area, or by an individual. We might talk of the 'vocabulary of politics', or indicate someone's complete separation from a concept by saying that it is 'not in their vocabulary'.

These senses have been with us since the eighteenth century, but when *vocabulary* was first introduced, in the sixteenth century, it meant something more tangible. The sixteenth century was the time of the Renaissance, when a flood of new words from classical and modern European languages entered English. The first *vocabularies* were lists of words with definitions and translations, and the term came to be especially applied to such a list in a grammar or reader for a foreign language. In Isaac Watts's *The Improvement of the Mind* (1741), we are advised that 'in order to improve our knowledge in general, or our acquaintance with any particular science, it is necessary that we should be furnished with vocabularies and dictionaries of several sorts'.

cuisine as known in the British Isles: chiefly French and (especially for pastries and desserts) Austro-German. Dishes from other countries were hardly covered, although there were a few honourable exceptions. (For example, Countess Morphy's 1937 *Good Food from Italy*, which provides the first instance of usage evidence for Italian dishes such as *cannelloni*, *panzanella*, *saltimbocca*, and *tortellini*.)

More exotic dishes were even less likely to be covered by recipe books, although there is one striking exception here. Families with Anglo-Indian connections and records of service brought home knowledge of *kedgeree*, *curries*, and other dishes, and many British women ran households in the Indian subcontinent. Works quoted by the *Oxford English Dictionary* include W. H. Dawe's 1888 *The Wife's Help to Indian Cookery*, which provides a quotation for *basmati rice*.

From the standpoint of 2010, it can be difficult to remember how different things were, although a salutary reminder was provided in the second leader of the *Times* of 2 March 2010. Celebrating the achievements of the British chef and cookery writer Rose Gray, who had died a few days before, the *Times* noted that between them she and Ruth Rogers (co-founder with her of the River Café) had turned England into a country where 'ciabatta, tortellini and pesto are part of the vocabulary'.

Looking at the dates at which cookery terms entered the language, and some of the titles of the books from which illustrative quotations were taken, gives some indication of the shift in which recipes from around the world (like their ingredients) moved from the unknown and exotic to the familiar. It also suggests how exploring language can take us on to a wider picture.

Chapter 7
Over to you: building up your own word files

THE purpose of this book has been to suggest ways in which we can interrogate words, and routes by which we may find our answers. At this point, it is over to you, the reader, to select your own questions, and build up your own records.

When the moon is blue

A news story from the beginning of January 2010 illustrates some of the ways in which you might build up your word files.

A range of headlines including 'Revellers wax lyrical over blue moon' (*Daily Express*, 1 January 2010, online edition) and 'A once-in-a-blue-moon New Year's Eve' (*New York Times* blog, 30 December 2009), centred on the full moon seen on New Year's Eve, 31 December 2009.

Even before getting to the stories, two expressions catch the eye: *blue moon* itself, and the longer phrase *once in a blue moon*. Obviously, whether you are looking at hard copy or online, the first thing to do is to read the chosen column carefully. However, if you have internet access, searching news stories for 'blue moon' is likely to offer you a range of choices. This in itself is helpful, as different articles may well provide further (or even contradictory) information, to be noted down for more detailed exploration.

Sifting through the coverage of 1 January 2010, we do in fact find two separate definitions for *blue moon*: that it is a moon which looks blue because of smoke or dust particles in the upper atmosphere (perhaps from a volcanic eruption), or that it is a name for the second full moon falling in a calendar month (as happened at the end of December 2009). The general consensus of the stories was that the moon seen on the 31st of December was described as 'blue' because of its date rather than its appearance. However, both definitions can be noted, together with a record of where the information has been found, and what extra relevant material occurs.

The full moon of New Year's Eve occasioned enormous interest (the *Independent* of 4 January 2010 reported that '"Blue moon" was the fourth most searched for topic' on Google over the previous seven days), so it is worth reading around articles to see what additional material can be found, even if you then feel that we want to test assertions made rather than taking them at face value.

The first thing, clearly, is to pin down the meaning of *blue moon*. As a first move, it makes sense to check what meanings are provided by whatever dictionaries (print or online) we have to hand. As both meanings come from a specialist area, astronomy, you will probably do well to consult a subject dictionary or encyclopedia as well as a dictionary of the language. (You should be alert as to where in the alphabetic sequence of the dictionary consulted *blue moon* is likely to be found. Ideally, of course, if covered under *moon*, there should be a cross reference to the place from *blue*, but it can be worth double-checking.)

Once the main senses given in the news articles have been substantiated, you can consider what extra material the news stories offer that does not appear and dictionary definitions found. Background information which invites further exploration suggestions that a moon with a blue tint was seen after the eruption of Krakatoa in 1883, and that the use of the term to mean the second full moon in a calendar month derives from a mistake. In the mid twentieth century, an explanation given by the American journal *Sky and Telescope* was said to have misinterpreted the use of the term in a Farmers' Almanack in use in Maine.

Online exploration of this claim revealed a press release from *Sky & Telescope* of 29 December 2009, headed 'Uh-Oh! A "Blue Moon" Ends the 00s'. This explained in some detail that in 1946 their writer, an amateur astronomer named James Hugh Pruett, had misunderstood how the term had been used in Maine (to mean the third full moon in a season containing four of them). Noting that the *American Heritage Dictionary* (2000) allows both definitions, the press release concludes that 'there's no turning back.' This is evidently correct, so *blue moon* offers an example of the way in which words and senses can accidentally extend their meaning.

Taking notes

Everyone will have their preferred way of building up word files, from a favourite notebook, through a card index, to a spreadsheet. What matters is that if you choose to record information, you do so in a way that is right for you, and that you can easily look up and add to (it is extremely unlikely that you will ever feel that there is no more to be said about a word or phrase). The traditional notebook is efficient and portable; on the other hand, a method which allows you to sort material according to different criteria (the spreadsheet) is extremely valuable. There is no reason, of course, why you should not combine the two: keep the notebook for initial notes, but transfer results to your spreadsheet when you feel that the time is right.

When you come down to your own record keeping, a key question arises: where do you want to file what you find? Both *blue* and *moon* are words with a long history, likely to occur in other contexts and phrases. You should therefore record the material in a way which will allow you to retrieve it by searching on either word. If you are using the notebook method, you could index *blue moon* under both words. If you use a spreadsheet, then you can have columns for main and secondary 'keywords' or index terms, so that at a later date you can look at all the items which include the word *blue*, and all those which include *moon*.

Exactly how much to record is another consideration. You are not writing a dictionary, or indeed a thesis on *blue moon*. What is kept is a matter of personal judgement, but a useful approach is to ask yourself how much of what you are thinking of recording is likely to be of real interest to you if you revisit the topic in a few months or years. With this particular instance, you can certainly say that the meanings of *blue moon* will always be relevant, and you are likely to want to find out how long the term has been in the language. You might want to know, as well, if there have been significant earlier uses by known writers, or in particular sources. The point at which the term caught your attention is worth having, and of course in this case there is the special interest of a particular context: the news event of a full moon occurring on New Year's Eve at the end of the first decade of the twenty-first century. However, you will need to decide exactly how much you want to record, given that a Google News search on 8 January 2010 turned up well over 3,500 hits. You should also take into account that you might want to add more material at a later date.

An initial record would cover the word or phrase under consideration, the meanings given, and a note of the circumstances and date at which the material has been recorded, either jotted down in a notebook or recorded electronically. A simple spreadsheet grid might look like this:

word/phrase	meaning (1)	meaning (2)	background
blue moon	moon that appears blue because of dust in upper atmosphere	second full moon in calendar month	news stories about 'blue moon' of New Year's Eve 2010; headlines included 'A "once-in-a-blue-moon" New Year's Eve', and 'Revellers wax lyrical over blue moon'

It will also be wise from the outset to get used to noting keywords, and a couple of extra columns could be added as follows:

word/ phrase	meaning (1)	meaning (2)	back- ground	keyword (1)	keyword (2)
blue moon	moon that appears blue because of dust in upper atmos- phere	second full moon in calendar month	news stories about 'blue moon' of New Year's Eve 2010; headlines included 'A "once-in- a-blue- moon" New Year's Eve', and 'Revellers wax lyrical over blue moon'	blue	moon

Beyond this, there may be other details to add. You have two main definitions, but are other meanings or contexts suggested in the news stories? In fact there are: one news story refers to the thought of the blue moon as 'inspiring baleful country and western ballads' (*Observer*, 3 January 2010).[1] *ABC News* of 31 December 2009 (http://abcnews.go.com), while noting that 'crooner Elvis Presley recorded both the melancholy ballad "Blue Moon" and the bluegrass hit "Blue Moon of Kentucky"', also pointed to another sense of *blue moon* which might be appropriate to celebration of New Year's Eve: 'Come happy hour, your barkeep might offer you a pint of "Blue Moon" beer or a flirty "Blue Moon" cocktail.'

It is appropriate to think quite hard about the form in which you want to keep records. Spreadsheets are convenient, but can easily become over-complex: not every word or phrase noted will have several senses, so adding a column for each possible sense of *blue moon* might mean that a good many entries had empty columns. To keep things straightforward, you could either have one extra column in which to note further possible senses, or simply enlarge the 'background information' column to make it the place in which this kind of thing is noted. As already suggested, you could simply record information in the traditional notebook, or even set up an alphabetical card index. There is no 'right way', only the way with which the word enthusiast feels comfortable, and which allows them to pursue their personal interest in language.

Once in a blue moon

So far we have looked at the literal meanings of *blue moon*, but much of the coverage (and the associated phrase *once in a blue moon*) has strong suggestions of it as typifying something which is so rare as to be almost incredible, or even ridiculous. You might now want to think about the origins of both expressions, which may well extend back beyond the factual astronomical senses at which we have been looking.

Again, before having recourse to dictionaries, it is wise to assemble any suggestions provided by our initial coverage. In this case, an *Observer* column of 3 January 2010, considering *blue moon* and *once in a blue moon*, suggests that the earliest usage is to be found in an anti-clerical pamphlet of 1528, criticizing the authoritative pronouncements of the Church: 'Yf they saye the mone is belewe / We must beleve that it is true.' This is clearly something to be pursued, although your notes should add that this is not a use of either phrase as we know them today, and that the meaning is different. In this quotation, to say that 'the moon is blue' is evidently presented as the statement of something different.

When you come across a quotation in modern journalism of an obscure historical source (with archaic spelling), it is highly likely that the material has come from a secondary work of reference. The sensible course is to consult the most likely work of reference for the historical record of a word or phrase: the *Oxford English Dictionary*. It is helpful, when searching such a large text, to have such a distinctive search term: a search for the string 'mone is belewe' across the text of illustrative quotations quickly brings up the couplet under the entry for *moon*.[2] The quotation illustrated an obsolete phrase *to say that the moon is blue*, meaning 'to believe an absurdity', which was later replaced by the variant *to believe that the moon is made of green cheese*.

At this point, you need to pause and consider the notes you are compiling, since these are related phrases rather than examples of *once in a blue moon* itself. The wording differs, and so does the sense: whether *blue* or made of *green cheese*, the moon in these expressions is seen as something absurdly impossible rather than rare. You should put down the new material, but also note that the 1528 quotation does not in fact provide the earliest use for *once in a blue moon* in the sense in which we have it. You need then to find the relevant *Oxford English Dictionary* entry.

Once in a blue moon appears in the *OED* under *once*, with the earliest (1547) form of the phrase appearing as *once in a moon*. (You might consider whether you should index *once*, or conclude that for your purposes *blue* and *moon* will be adequate.) The meaning, quite simply, is 'rarely, exceptionally'.

It is perhaps not surprising that headline writers and columnists used *once in a blue moon* in wordplay around the New Year of 2010. In one instance of serendipity it was deployed to describe a unique finding:

> Rare things happen once in a blue moon, and on New Year's Day a blue moon, coupled with an exceptionally low tide, uncovered a long-sought treasure in the frozen wastes of Antarctica: one of the world's earliest aeroplanes, entombed in ice for decades.
> —in *Independent* (www.independent.co.uk) 4 January 2010

For the person interested in social, cultural, and historical links with language, the association of an actual 'blue moon' with so rare an event might itself be worthy of record.

The *Observer* column already referred to opened up enticing avenues by bringing *once in a blue moon* together with other phrases meaning 'seldom or never':

Having looked at the actual frequency of occurrence of a calendrical 'blue moon', the columnist concluded:

> The lesson learnt is perhaps that once in a blue moon is a
> far shorter time than waiting for pigs to fly and occurs
> long before we reach the twelfth of never.
> —in *Observer* (www.guardian.co.uk) 3 January 2010

This presents another challenge as you build up your files: how should you deal with other interesting phrases with the same meaning? Should you make separate entries for *when pigs fly* and *the twelfth of never*, while ensuring that each of them has a note linking it to *once in a blue moon*? This would seem advisable, since both of them have the feel of established (and indeed colourful) phrases which would in themselves be worth investigating.

Blue cheese?

Once more, a single phrase can take you on a journey, and demonstrate how important it is that you should be able to add to your initial files at a later date. We have already seen that while *once in a blue moon* dates from the mid nineteenth century, the *Oxford English Dictionary* entry for *moon* gives *to say that the moon is blue* as an obsolete and earlier variant of *to believe that the moon is made of green cheese*, both meaning 'to believe an absurdity'. You can note these extensions, but also be ready for further developments.

In June 2008, a *New York Times* column entitled 'Kiplin' vs. Palin' quoted in detail from Rudyard Kipling's poem 'The Gods of the Copybook Headings', in which, as the columnist points out, Kipling uses the proverbial wisdom of copybooks to counter attractive but delusive beliefs. The 'Gods of the Copybook Headings' remain solidly in touch with inconvenient facts, and immune to spin:

> They denied that the Moon was Stilton
> They denied she was even Dutch.
> —Rudyard Kipling 'The Gods of the Copybook
>   Headings' (1919)

The lines would not turn up in any search based on *blue* or *green*, and could not be quoted in a dictionary as usage evidence for the phrases we have looked at, but for someone interested in language they are relevant. It is only in the light of the phrases at which we have been looking that they make sense. It would therefore be entirely valid to add a note about Kipling's poem to your file on *once in a blue moon*.

Fruitful sources

Up to this point, we have been talking about records of individual searches, but of course it can also be useful to keep notes of the most promising sources found. Once more you can choose your preferred format—a paragraph in a notebook, or a bookmarked website—but in any case it is often useful to keep a note of particular specialities. At its simplest, this might mean noting down which particular dictionary has been most helpful in exploring a given aspect of language, but it could also mean keeping a record of some of the functions provided by a resource. To take one example, in the foregoing pages we have been looking at the *OED* entry for *moon*, which unsurprisingly is a long entry. In finding your way about it, we might decide to use the function buttons for 'Quotations' and 'Date chart', which will present you with an entry that suppresses the actual quotations, but offers a timeline for each sense. If you are skimming through the entry, and perhaps want to look quickly at its phrases and compounds, this offers a helpful way of seeing a summary, while retaining a grip on the chronology.

You might also want to note another way of using the *OED*: as a general resource for evidence of the historical language. A simple search will search the whole text of the dictionary, but you can easily restrict the field at which you are looking. If you choose to search 'quotation text', you will be looking only at material provided as illustrative usage evidence: in other words, a database of the historical language.

The *OED* website offers a wide variety of ways in which to search its material and filter the evidence, and other dictionary websites and CD-ROMs similarly offer extra functionality. Your choice of the function which offers most to you in trying to find the answer to a particular question will vary, but it is always worth noting which functions you have found especially effective, and why.

When thinking about resources, it is inevitable that the first category at which you look is that of dictionaries, closely followed by thesauruses—in other words, resources which are specifically targeted at the recording and analysis of language. However, it is also likely that you will find useful material in reference sources which spread a wider net. Someone interested in American English of the nineteenth century will find invaluable the *Making of America* site: this provides electronic access to a library of 'primary sources in American social history from the antebellum period through reconstruction'. Again, your favourite sources will depend on your particular interests, but we will all have books or websites to which we turn naturally, because we have already made successful use of them.

Knowing the language

As we have seen, dictionaries and language resources have their own jargon. It might be helpful to make a note of terms which are important because they are used in providing guidance to a reader, but which may not be readily familiar. For example, one of the options for searching the *OED* text is to search 'lemmas': an expression with a very specific meaning, which is not necessarily part of our everyday vocabulary. You might need to consult a dictionary to discover that the meaning of lemma here is 'a word or phrase defined in the dictionary'. When searching 'lemmas' in *OED*, you are searching all the headwords together with the phrases, compounds, and derivatives which are found within the main entries.

Watching the news

Blue moon was an example of a term which caught the eye because it figured in a news story. Some of the coverage provided information (or speculation) about the term, and we were

godless

In June 2009, the British press reported on a summer camp for children to be run on humanist and atheist principles, which would provide a 'godless alternative' for summer activities. *Godless* here was clearly being used in a neutral and literal sense, which prompted exploration of the degree to which this was in fact standard usage.

Investigation shows that current and historical dictionary coverage of *godless* tends to the pejorative: single-word alternatives include 'impious' and 'wicked', and a typical sentence from current English is given as 'the godless forces of Communism'. Earlier uses (the word goes back to the first half of the sixteenth century) include Milton in *Paradise Lost* (1667): 'Behold God's indignation on these Godless poured.' Coin collectors call 1849 florins which omitted the words *Dei Gratia* 'By the grace of God' from Queen Victoria's titles *godless florins*. We may ask whether the usage in our 'godless alternative' might represent an attempt to reclaim or reposition the word.

then able to pursue it further ourselves. However, another way in which to use news stories is to watch for, and keep (by cutting out, copying, or bookmarking web pages) stories which feature language in general. Depending again on your particular interests, you could decide to collect news stories on regional varieties of English, slang, etymology, spelling, or pronunciation. Once you have gathered material over a period of months, you can go back over it, and see if there are details of information that we would like to add to your own files, or stories which complement one another. At times, you may well find that an account will highlight an approach to language that will add further interest to future explorations.

Over to you

Everyone, as we have said, will have their own approach. One person will enjoy compiling detailed files, while at the opposite end of the spectrum, another will be satisfied by the interest of a particular word-hunt: tracking a word or phrase through texts or centuries, or exploring the fascinating side paths that are likely to open up. (The final chapter, 'Oranges are not the only fruit', offers an extended illustration of where a simple question can take you.) But whatever your preferences, once you start it is probably inevitable that you will find that you have begun to have your own favourite resources and ways of working, whether or not you choose to record them formally.

skulduggery

Skulduggery is one of those words which sound as though they might be dated or archaic, but which are clearly alive and well in the language. Between 2009 and 2010, the word made numerous appearances in the news, frequently in the worlds of politics, finance, and sport (collocations such as *political skulduggery*, *financial skulduggery*, and even *Olympic skulduggery* were all recorded). It appears to be a word of choice when misdoing in a particular field is being alleged: *accusations of skulduggery* is a well-established expression. And while the term does have a faintly humorous air, the contexts in which such accusations are made are clearly serious.

It can be interesting, in a case like this, to look back at the word's earlier history: to what degree (if any) has usage changed? In fact, when we look at *OED*, *skulduggery* seems remarkably constant. The first quotation on record, from an 1867 American source, refers to 'the mysterious term "scull-duggery", used to signify political or other trickery'. The latest quotation, from 1980 (this section of the alphabet has not yet been revised), from the London *Times*, runs, 'Watergate was such a sensational piece of skulduggery.' Both quotations are entirely in tune with usage today, which prompts the thought that the stability of the term may result from *skulduggery*'s being a necessary item of vocabulary: there is nothing else that quite expresses what is, perhaps regrettably, an enduring concept.

Afterword

I N the early stages of planning this book, I decided to follow the paths opened up by a single question to see for myself where interrogating one word might lead me. The following chapter, which illustrates the varying routes leading from *satsuma*, is the result: an illustration of some of the possibilities of exploration.

Chapter 8

'Oranges are not the only fruit': where a single question can lead

I N 2009, a friend told me that his daughter, then working in Japan, had been struck by the name of Satsuma province. She wondered about its connection (if any) with the satsumas found on Western fruit counters—not least because the term *satsuma* did not appear to be used for the fruit in Japan. The answer to her question led on to a whole range of further possible questions. The result, endorsing Jeanette Winterson's phrase[1], illustrates the purpose of this book: to show in how many ways we can interrogate the words we encounter every day, and how one question naturally leads to another.

The first step in investigating *satsuma* was naturally to consult dictionaries of current English, and from this process some initial information was assembled. Dictionary etymologies agreed that the fruit ('a tangerine of a hardy loose-skinned variety, originally grown in Japan', in the definition of the *Oxford Dictionary of English*; a seedless thin-skinned fruit of 'any of several cold-tolerant cultivated mandarin trees', according to *Merriam-Webster's Collegiate Dictionary*) had been named after the former Japanese province of Satsuma, in the south-western quarter of Kyushu island. As the name of the fruit, it had appeared in English in the late nineteenth century, a period during which *Satsuma* had already been used to designate a kind of cream-coloured Japanese pottery[2].

Consultation of the entry for *satsuma* in the *Oxford English Dictionary* narrowed the date of introduction: the first quotation for the fruit was dated 1882, and came from a reference in the *Proceedings* of the 18th Session of the American Pomological Society to 'One [variety of tangerine] from Japan called Satsuma'. The quotation suggests that (at least within a limited circle) the name was already known, and examination of later quotations in the *OED* entry supports this. A mid-twentieth-century source is quoted as attestation for a much more precise date: 'The Satsuma was first introduced into the United States in 1876 by Dr George R. Hall' (Webber and Batchelor *The Citrus Industry*, 1943).

These clues suggested an avenue for further online research. Trying Google News Archive for the words 'satsuma' and 'fruit', and limiting the date range to sources between 1876 and 1882, turned up a number of sources relating to pottery, and one which does in fact relate to the fruit. This is from an Australian paper, the *Maitland Mercury, and Hunter River General Advertiser*, for 28 May 1881. Under 'Miscellaneous Items' there is a report on 'A New Variety of Orange', which cites a report from the *Sun and Press* of Jacksonville, Florida, of an orange recently introduced into that state. It had been named *satsuma*, after the main city of the island of Kiusiu [Kyushu]

> ...by the request of Mrs General Van Valkenburg[3]. The trees of this variety and species were introduced into

Satsuma

SECOND EDITION 1989

[Pronunciation] [Spellings] [Etymology] [Quotations] [Date chart]

(sætsjuma, now (esp. in sense 2) freq. sæts uma) Also **Satzuma**. [The name of a province in the island of Kiusiu, Japan.]

1. Used *attrib.* in *Satsuma ware*, a kind of cream-coloured Japanese pottery. Also *absol.*

1872 W. CHAFFERS *Keramic Gallery* I. Pl. 99 Satsuma-Ware Bottle... Satsuma Bowl. **1875** AUDSLEY & BOWES *Keramic Art Japan* II. Pl. xi, Three vases of middle period Satsuma Faïence..good representatives of a style of decoration but seldom met with in Satsuma ware. **1880** T. W. CUTLER *Grammar Jap. Ornament* 16 Modern Satsuma is largely decorated at Tokio and elsewhere. **1909** M. DIVER *Candles in Wind* ix. 86 Roses..filling every available bowl, even the sacred Satsuma. **1974** SAVAGE & NEWMAN *Illustr. Dict. Ceramics* 255 True Satsuma is comparatively rare outside Japan.

2. (Freq. with lower-case initial.) A small tangerine belonging to a variety of *Citrus reticulata* so called; also, the variety itself. Also *attrib.* as **Satsuma orange.**

1882 E. S. HART in *Proc. 18th Session Amer. Pomological Soc. 1881* 67/1 One [variety of tangerine] from Japan called Satsuma, bore a temperature of 16°. **1905** *Flora & Sylva* III. 66/1 Satsuma, an early fruiting Mandarine. **1909** *Circular Bureau Plant Industry U.S. Dept. Agric.* XLVI (*title*) The limitation of the Satsuma orange to trifoliate-orange stock. **1922** [see MIKAN]. **1926** H. H. HUME *Cultivation of Citrus Fruits* xxix. 477 Satsuma oranges are susceptible to the disease. **1943** WEBER & BATCHELOR *Citrus Industry* I. v. 551 The Satsuma was first introduced into the United States in 1876 by Dr. George R. Hall... It is characteristic of Satsuma fruits that although they mature and fill with juice..the rind frequently remains green or shows only slightly colored. **1967** [see CLEMENTINE]. **1980** 'M. YORKE' *Scent of Fear* vii. 64 She bought..some tangerines—or satsumas, as they were called nowadays.

Oxford English Dictionary entry for *satsuma*, showing a date chart for the entry.

127

Florida by Dr George R. Hall in 1876, and also by
Mr Van Valkenburg in 1878. The trees were imported
direct from Japan.

The article went on to give a full description of trees and
fruit, and prophesied (correctly) that the new fruit would
'doubtless take high rank for table and dessert'.[4]

What other names are there?

Those interested in the history of citrus fruits could use this
extra information to explore further what was happening in
Florida in the late 1870s. However, the basic information
already culled from dictionaries supplied a number of other
starting points for further discovery. *Satsuma* is one of a
number of names for a particular kind of fruit, and the entries consulted had already supplied a couple of further
names: *orange* (obviously), and *tangerine*. A natural question
then was, what other words belong to the set of words
comprising names for a kind of orange, and how can we find
them?

An immediate way was to utilize the resources already employed, and see what related names were suggested by the
entry for *satsuma*, either in the body of the definition, the etymology, or the illustrative quotations. Mention of relevant
names may be found either as part of the text ('a tangerine of
a hardy loose-skinned variety'), or as direct cross-references
('see CLEMENTINE'). The *Oxford English Dictionary* prints the
range of quotations which comprise its historical evidence
(in the case of *satsuma*, from 1882 to 1980), and it was worth

reading through the material in case it referred to other possible types of fruit.

The section of illustrative quotations for *satsuma* in *OED* has one implicit reference, and two direct cross-references to be followed up. The first of these, a quotation from 1905, supplies the name *mandarin*:

> 1905 *Flora & Sylva* III. 66/1 Satsuma, an early fruiting Mandarine.

After this, we find

> 1922 [see MIKAN].
> 1967 [see CLEMENTINE].

Direct cross-references in a quotation block mean that the word in question is to be found in the quotation for another word, which may not necessarily be related to the initial entry, so these two had to be followed up to see whether the new headwords did in fact belong to the relevant set of words. *Clementine* is likely to be recognized as belonging to the group before the definition ('a variety of small orange') has been found, but *mikan* may well not be familiar, since it is not to be found in dictionaries of current English[5]. However, the *OED* entry confirms its relevance as another name for a type of citrus fruit 'originally cultivated in Japan; *esp.* a variety of mandarin orange, a satsuma'.

All these fruits are a variety of *orange*, so an immediate way of adding to the set was to look at the full entry for the superordinate term. The *OED* definition for *orange* includes the information that there are two main groupings of the fruit, named respectively *Seville orange* or *bitter orange* on the one hand, and *sweet orange* or *China orange* on the other. Beyond this, the entry provides a list of other terms:

> *Bergamot, blood, Jaffa, mandarin, navel, Portugal, Satsuma, tangerine orange,* etc.: see the first element.

All this material could be found by consulting dictionaries in the traditional way: by taking a (substantial) volume from its shelf. However, online resources now offer further possibilities. When the full text of *OED* online is searched for *satsuma*, the entries returned include *Nagami*, a term from Japanese which was first recorded in English (in 1935) as the full form *Nagami kumquat*. As well as adding to the list of Japanese words in this context, the reference also provided the word *kumquat* to look up directly. Searching for entries including *tangerine* returned *naartjie*, a South African name for a type of tangerine or mandarin orange. A further refined search of definitions for '"citrus fruit" + "orange"' added *ortanique, tangelo,* and *Ugli* to the tally. Overall, a substantial range of words had been amassed. The next question was, how best to begin to explore their stories?

When was it first used?

When looking at a group of related words, it can be of interest to note down dates of recorded first use, to get an overall view of the chronology[6].

Orange, the overarching term, is unsurprisingly the oldest by some centuries: the first occurrence given by *OED* is in a fourteenth-century glossary, as the translation of the Latin *Citrangulum pomum*. By the early sixteenth century, the word

Date range	Fruit
Late Middle English	orange
1600–49	mikan
1650–99	bergamot (orange), kumquat
1700–49	Portugal (orange)
1750–99	mandarin (orange), naartjie
1800–49	tangerine
1850–99	Jaffa, navel (orange), satsuma
1900–49	clementine, Nagami, ortanique, tangelo, Ugli
1950–99	
2000–	

was in general use (although the spelling of the time is unfamiliar to us): there is a reference by a correspondent in the *Paston Letters* to 'Halfe a hondyrd orrygys'.

The next introduction, *mikan*, is first recorded in a journal entry for the early seventeenth century:

> 1618 R. COCKS *Diary*[7] 12 Feb. (1883) II. 14 Pasquall Benita came from Langasaque to Firando and brought me a present of *coiebos*, *micanas*, and peares.

Just over 80 years later (in 1699) *kumquats* and *bergamots* made their first appearance in the language. *Portugal oranges* and *mandarin oranges* were added in the eighteenth century, *tangerines*, *navel oranges*, and *Jaffa oranges* in the nineteenth century, and finally in the twentieth century a cluster of terms including *clementine*, *ortanique*, and *tangelo*.

Where does that come from?

Exploration of etymologies for a number of these terms revealed several categories of name origin. *Satsuma*, as we have seen, comes from a place name, and so does *tangerine*. This variety of fruit was exported from the Moroccan seaport of *Tangier*, which in the nineteenth century was still known as *Tanger*. *Clementine* is a direct borrowing from another language (French *clémentine*), and two of the other names on our list are hybrids. *Ortaniques* are a cross between oranges and tangerines, and the name comes from a blend of *orange*, *tangerine*, and *unique*. The *tangelo* was produced by crossing the *tangerine* with another citrus fruit, the *pomelo*[8], and the name reflects this. The trademark name of the mottled green and yellow *Ugli* fruit, hybrid of a grapefruit and a tangerine, is a deliberate alteration of the word *ugly*.

Some of the names on our list have a more complex history, and can be traced back through several languages; they may also convey more of the way in which the fruit in question was seen. The name *orange* comes from Old French *orenge* (in the phrase *pomme d'orenge*, meaning 'fruit of the orange tree'), and goes back through Persian to Arabic *nāranj*. The detailed etymology of the *Oxford English Dictionary* suggests that the initial *o-* may come from the name of *Orange* in Provence, or that the colour of the fruit may have prompted an association with *or* 'gold'. *Mandarin* comes to us (somewhat surprisingly) through Swedish: the explanation is that it is first recorded in a translation from that language, Johann Forster's 1777 translation of Pehr Osbeck's *Voyage to China and the East Indies*. The most likely suggestion is that the colour of the fruit was associated with the yellow silk robes worn by Chinese mandarins, although it is also possible that the name carried the implication that it was a particularly choice fruit. The *kumquat* gets its name from Chinese (Cantonese) *kam kwat*, 'little orange'. *Naartjie*, an Afrikaans word, comes ultimately from the Tamil word for a citrus tree. The first element of *mikan* comes from Middle Chinese *mitsu* 'honey', and may ultimately be linked with the Indo-European base of *mead*, the name for an alcoholic drink of fermented honey and water going back to the Anglo-Saxon period. Stories of word origins can take us not only across the centuries, but across the globe.

Poetry and prose

We had already seen (with *mikan* in Richard Cocks's Japanese diary, and *mandarin* in the account of Pehr Osbeck's eastern voyages) that early uses of names for citrus fruit are likely to be found in accounts of travels. It was then a natural question to ask what examples are to be found in what might be regarded as more literary sources, and an immediate way to look for examples was to consult a dictionary of quotations. This offered (for *orange*) examples from two well-known seventeenth-century poets. George Herbert, writing in the first half of the seventeenth century, saw the orange as an emblem of fruitfulness:

> Oh that I were an orange tree,
> That busy plant!
> Then I should ever laden be,
> And never want

> Some fruit for him that dressed me.
> —'Employment: he that is weary, let him sit' (1633)

Twenty years later, Andrew Marvell also evoked the image of fruit growing on the tree, in words which emphasize the glowing colour[9] of the fruit:

> He hangs in shades the orange bright,
> Like golden lamps in a green night.
> —'Bermudas' (*c.*1653)

It is of course possible, through Google Books[10] or perhaps (if you have access to it) the Chadwyck-Healey *Literature Online* database, to search the work of a specific author for particular words. Looking at terms in use by the sixteenth century, it would be natural to ask whether they appear in Shakespeare's plays. The candidates from our current list would be *mikan* and *orange*.

It is probably not surprising that, while *mikan* is not found, *orange* has a number of hits. Scanning the results by eye, we find one particular reference that looks worth investigating further. In Shakespeare's *Much Ado about Nothing*, Beatrice teases Claudio by saying that he is 'neither sad, nor sick, nor merry, nor well: but civil, count, civil as an orange, and something of that jealous complexion'. An annotation from a scholarly edition explains that *civil* here is a play on *Seville*, the Spanish city noted as a source for bitter oranges—so someone likened to such a fruit is seen as both sweet and sour. If we go back to *OED* and look at the entry for Seville, we find *Seville orange* recorded from the late sixteenth century, and first appearing in just this wordplay: Thomas Nashe's *Strange Newes, of the Intercepting Certaine Letters, and Convoy of*

Verses (1592) 'For the order of my life, it is as ciuil as a ciuil orenge.'

On the move

The longer a word is embedded in the language, the more likely it is to develop transferred or figurative uses, as we have already seen in the development of colour terms, and the wordplay indicated above. It was therefore worth as a start looking at the *OED* entry for *orange* in this light. The section for phrases had the children's game *oranges and lemons*, recorded from the early nineteenth century, and, perhaps more interestingly, the seventeenth-century *to suck* (or *squeeze*) *the orange*, meaning 'to extract all profit or vitality from something'.

The idea of used and discarded fruit has been a potent one for a long time.[11] In the first part of the nineteenth century, the statesman George Canning (1770–1827) wrote[12], 'For fame, it is a squeezed orange; but for public good there is something to do.'[13] In more recent times, Julie Burchill opined, 'Beauty contests are a sucked orange, much too redundant to boil blood.'[14] A more general search of news archive sources for *squeezed orange* and *sucked orange* revealed a number of further uses, including a much-quoted source on the sale of Alaska to America by Russia in 1867, which apparently took the unenthusiastic view that 'Russia has sold us a sucked orange.'[15]

In checking for further possibilities, one strategy is to identify fuller terms for searching more widely. The first sense of the *OED*'s entry for *orange* gave *China orange* as a fuller name for the *sweet orange* (as contrasted with the *Seville*, or *bitter*, *orange*).

A full-text search across the dictionary for *China orange* returned a hit under the entry for *Lombard-street*, defined as

> The name of a street in London, so called because originally occupied by Lombard bankers, and still containing many of the principal London banks.

The entry goes on to explain that from this the term came to be used for '"money market"; the body of financiers'. The material sought, while not explicitly cued, was found among the quotations given to illustrate uses of *Lombard Street*.

The phrase *Lombard Street to a China orange* is found in a number of instances from 1815, with a quotation from the late nineteenth century offering a particularly clear use:

> We describe the betting upon a moral certainty as being
> All Lombard-street to a China orange.
> *Evening Standard* 9 November 1892

The *China orange* in this figure of speech represents something so common as to be virtually worthless (in direct contrast to the wealth concentrated in *Lombard Street*), an idea that can be linked to the thought of a fruit sucked or squeezed dry, and thrown away.

Summing up

The word *orange* has been part of the language since the Middle Ages, just as the fruit it denotes has been part of our culture. The *OED* lists *orange girl* (from 1764) and *orange wench* (from 1664, in the diary of Samuel Pepys) among terms for those 'employed in the orange trade'. Searching the text of the *Oxford Dictionary of National Biography* for the terms adds considerably to the picture of the orange in the seventeenth century: the youthful Nell Gwyn, later actress and mistress of Charles II, seems to have got her start in the King's Theatre 'where Nell apparently became an orange girl, selling oranges to the theatregoers in 1663'[16] (making an orange the equivalent of the modern-day tub of ice cream, or bag of popcorn). A search across the same text for *orange wench* is even more productive, since it provides a fuller version of the Pepys quotation cited in *OED*. The life in this case is that of Frances Talbot, née Jennings, elder sister of Sarah, Duchess of Marlborough, and records an escapade of her youth:

> In February 1665 Pepys recorded that she went to the theatre disguised 'like an orange wench, and went up and down and cried oranges; till falling down, or by some such accident, though in the evening, her fine shoes were discovered, and she put to a great deal of shame'.
> —*Oxford Dictionary of National Biography* (online edition), 'Frances Talbot'

By the nineteenth century, there is further evidence from *ODNB* of oranges being readily available, since in 1870 the fifth Marquess Townshend, social reformer and would-be legislator, saw orange peel as a distinct threat:

> His Metropolitan Regulations Bill (1870) addressed matters of life and limb in London's streets: it sought to create an offence of throwing or dropping orange peel on footways (based on statistics of accidents caused by treading on peel).
> —*Oxford Dictionary of National Biography* (online edition), 'John Villiers Stuart Townshend'

It is fair to add that orange peel was not the only danger identified in the bill; others included 'the too rapid driving of horses'; it also sought

> To stop the dangerous and improper practice of females cleaning outside windows above the level of the ground floor; and to prohibit the placing of flower pots in precarious positions.
> —*Oxford Dictionary of National Biography* (online edition),
> 'John Villiers Stuart Townshend'

However, although today a reference to *orange peel* does not have the figurative power of *banana skin* (as in P. G. Wodehouse's reference to 'Treading upon Life's banana skins'[17]), a little investigation can turn up literal and figurative references to its dangers in the previous century. The *Westminster Gazette* of June 1899, reflecting on the fall of the French government, noted that one journal writing on the subject had compared 'the events of Sunday simply to a piece of orange-peel on which M. Dupuy slipped'. Thirty years before, a Dickens character had introduced himself with a bitter reference to the 'surgeon's friend'. Mr Grimwig in *Oliver Twist* (1869) tells his friend Mr Brownlow and the young Oliver: 'I've been lamed by orange-peel once, and orange-peel will be my death at last.'

Satsuma has had much less time to make an impact, and less opportunity: the word, unlike *orange*, is not a generic term under which a much wider grouping of different fruits is subsumed. It also, as we have seen, has to share its place in the language with an almost bewildering range of names for citrus fruits. Nevertheless, it has its own history, and it has also provided the starting point for a number of paths through the language.

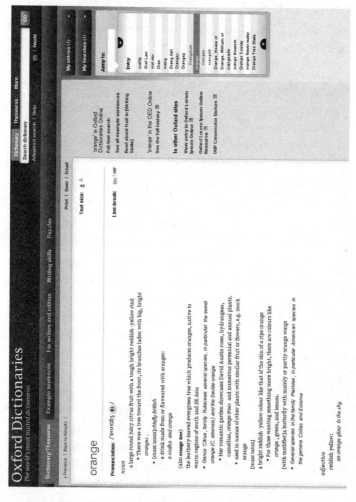

Oxford Dictionaries Online website, showing a search for *orange*.

Appendix

Pathways of English

ALL living languages evolve: new words and ways of expression are added and developed; some older ones drop out of use. English is no exception: from its inception the base language has been augmented by derivation from existing words, compounding of one word with another, addition of prefixes and suffixes, imitation of a natural sound, and arbitrary coinage. At the same time, words disappear: sometimes replaced by alternative expressions, sometimes because the thing they designate is no longer familiar or spoken of, or simply because they gradually become old-fashioned and lose their force to communicate. Changes like this occur through the centuries, but against this background it is possible to mark particular periods of English.

In the beginning

The earliest 'English' that we have is the language developed in Britain following the invasion and settlement of the Germanic Anglo-Saxon peoples in the fifth and sixth centuries. All these invaders spoke a form of Germanic language (which in their continental relatives ultimately gave rise to modern German, Dutch, and the Scandinavian languages). Approximately fifteen hundred years later, many of the words they used remain, with their original meaning, in our twenty-first-century language. (Some words which first appeared in Old English did not immediately develop what we now recognize as their main sense. Thus, *road* in Old English meant 'a journey on horseback' or 'a foray'; the sense 'a wide way leading from one place to another' is not recorded until the late sixteenth century.)

Many of the words are recognizable as designating familiar things from the immediate world: animals (*bird, cow, fox, lamb*), crops (*corn, oats*), flowers (*clover, daisy*), food (*bread, meat*), people (*child, father, lady, man, woman*), parts of the body (*chin, thumb*), weapons and technology (*nail, sword*), the weather (*rain, snow*), social and political organization (*church, king*), numbers (*five, seven*), and time (*day, night, year*).

The Celtic peoples who preceded the Anglo-Saxons left a comparatively small mark on the language of the invaders: their vocabulary was superseded rather than absorbed. However, a few words were adopted into Old English, and have come forward to today (often as the element of a place name). One of these is *brock*, the name for a badger ('Tommy Brock' is the name of the badger in Beatrix Potter's 1912 children's story *The Tale of Mr Tod*). *Brock*, which comes from a Celtic base, is preserved in the name of the Hampshire town of *Brockenhurst*. *Combe*, meaning a deep hollow or valley, also goes back to a Celtic original. It occurs from early times in place names from the south of England, many of which survive today (*Batscombe, Harting Combe, Southcombe*).

When looking at words from the Anglo-Saxon period, we need to remember that while Old English was a Germanic language, which often found a native equivalent for foreign words and phases, it was also (like modern English) able to borrow and absorb non-Germanic words. Latin was the language of the Church, and it is hardly surprising to find that an 'Old English' word like *abbot*, coming in from ecclesiastical Latin, derives from Greek and ultimately from Aramaic.

We should also be aware that while the Anglo-Saxon invasions began in the middle of the fifth century, the earliest *written* form of the language that we have dates from the seventh century.

Old English words still in use today

alderman	goose	oats
ale	hammer	pound
bird	hand	queen
black	harvest	rain
blood	hawk	salt
bread	heaven	sea
bride	heifer	seven
calf	hell	silk
child	iron	snake
chin	ivy	snow
church	jowl	soap
clothes	kettle	song
clover	key	sparrow
corn	king	sword
cow	lady	teach
daisy	lamb	ten
day	laugh	thief
death	life	thigh
deer	loaf	thread
drink	man	thumb
eat	meat	thunder
eye	mistletoe	Thursday
fat	Monday	tongue
father	mouse	vixen
feather	murder	walk
field	nail	wife
five	name	woman
fox	night	worm
glass	nose	year
god	oak	youth
gold	oar	

Viking invaders

Between the eighth and the eleventh centuries, many parts of northwestern Europe were subject to raids, and then settlement, by seafaring Norse pirates and traders. From the middle of the ninth century, large numbers of Norsemen settled in Britain, especially in the north and east of the country: by the mid tenth century, the Viking leader Erik Bloodaxe had been accepted as ruler of a kingdom centred on York. From the late Old English period, the word *Danelaw* was used to designate what the *Shorter Oxford English Dictionary* defines as: 'The Danish law . . . in force over that part of England which was occupied by Danes from the 9th to the 11th cents.' (The current sense of 'the part of northern and eastern England over which this law prevailed' was first used in historical accounts of the period written in the nineteenth century.)

The North Germanic speech of the invaders (Old Norse) exerted a strong Scandinavian influence on the language of the Anglo-Saxons. Borrowings which we still use today include some of our most familiar words, such as *egg* (which replaced the related Old English *ey*), *guest* (which similarly had a related Old English predecessor), *knife*, *take*, and *they*. Others, reflecting the geographical distribution of the settlers, are now chiefly known as part of northern dialect, for example *beck* (a brook or rivulet), *dreich* ('dreary, bleak', although originally it meant 'patient, long-suffering'), and *elding* ('fuel').

As Old Norse and Old English were both Germanic languages, they shared many features, and so it is not always possible to be clear about the precise ancestry of a given word. In fact, the substantial part of Norse influence did not make its way through to the written language until the medieval period.

Words from Old Norse

anger	creek	loose
arrow	cur	mistake
bairn	dove	odd
bark (of a tree)	draught	rotten
beaker	dyke	scare
beck (a stream)	egg	slight
bracken	give	take
brink	guest	they
cart	hank	thrive
club	knife	whirl

The Norman Conquest

1066 is a watershed. The Norman Conquest brought to England political, social, and cultural changes, through the power of a ruling elite whose language (Anglo-Norman) was French rather than Germanic. In the following centuries (what is known as the Middle English period), the language naturally changed significantly. Old English was an inflectional language, depending on distinctive word endings for grammatical meaning. Middle English, by contrast, followed the system that we have today, with meaning expressed through word order. The ease with which borrowings from other languages were absorbed increased greatly, with a host of words from French and Latin becoming part of the English language.

Foreign borrowings in the medieval period: French and Latin

author	Bible	chamber
banker	blue	champion
beverage	certain	channel

chimney	gutter	sanctuary
city	herb	soldier
compass	liquor	spirit
corner	manner	stranger
country	marble	tavern
cousin	nature	tiger
cuckoo	onion	treacle
dame	parliament	vessel
danger	pearl	voyage
dromedary	pen	warranty
eager	purgatory	warrior
feud	quarter	
gentle	remember	

A changing world: Early Modern English

During the late medieval and early modern period, the form of English that developed in the London region had an increasing influence on the wider language in the country at large. When in the fifteenth century this was coupled with the new technology of printing, the result was a growing recognition of a London standard which was seen as the language of educated people—as distinct from the regional varieties known and spoken in other areas. This was to be the language we still hear at a performance of Shakespeare, or perhaps in a reading from the 1611 Authorized Version of the Bible. However, that is not to say that all words which did not remain in the mainstream language were lost entirely.

Words from Old and Middle English surviving in the later language as dialect

attercop ('a spider')
carl ('a countryman')
chesil ('gravel, shingle')

Childermas ('Holy Innocents' Day, 28 December')
cloam ('mud, clay')

culver ('a pigeon')

emmet ('an ant')

forold ('grow old')

frosk ('a frog')

gleed ('an ember, a live coal')

gripple ('miserly')

hield ('lean, incline')

lewth ('warmth')

Lide ('the month of March')

mixen ('a dunghill')

muckle ('great in size')

nesh ('soft')

ouzel ('a blackbird')

rearmouse ('a bat')

rithe ('a small stream')

ruddock ('a robin')

seely ('happy, lucky')

shippon ('a cattle shed')

thirl ('a hole')

threshel ('a flail')

treen ('made of wood')

unwemmed ('immaculate')

vinny ('mouldy')

wark ('a pain')

wonning ('a dwelling place')

yarm ('scream')

Even in this list, however, some words have a more tenacious hold on a wider currency. *Chesil* is likely to be known from the name of *Chesil Beach*, the long shingle beach in southern England off the Dorset coast. *Emmet* is used in Cornwall as a word for a tourist or holidaymaker. Anyone attending a performance of Shakespeare's *A Midsummer Night's Dream* will hear Titania's orders to her fairy attendants to 'war with *rearmice* for their leathern wings, To make my small elves coats'. *Treen* in the twentieth century came to be used in the antique trade as a collective term for small wooden domestic objects. Dorset Blue *Vinny* is one of the cheeses which John Cleese was unable to buy in Monty Python's 'Cheese Shop' sketch.

William Caxton (*c*.1422–91) printed the first book in English in 1474. In the following century, the impact of the Renaissance saw a 'rebirth' of learning, under the influence of classical models. Greek and Latin were the languages of scholarship, and they contributed a range of new vocabulary to designate new concepts, often providing key terms in specialist subject areas such as medicine (*arthritis, physiology*) and politics (*democracy, oligarchy*), which are now part of our everyday language.

At the same time, an increasing number of terms from modern European languages was added to the language: for example, *duomo* (for an Italian cathedral), *madrigal*, and *pavane* (a dance) from Italian, and *armada* from Spanish.

Words from Greek and Latin first recorded in the sixteenth century

abdomen	caesura	maximum
abortion	capitulation	metaphysics
aconite	catastrophe	metropolis
aedile	censor	oligarchy
ambrosia	chorus	panacea
anarchy	cube	philippic
antirrhinum	despot	phrase
aorta	diabetes	physiology
apostrophe	dogma	sarcasm
appendix	ellipsis	scene
archetype	encyclopedia	symmetry
architect	enigma	tragic
arthritis	hero	vocabulary
basilica	laconic	zealot
binomial	Lethe	

Not all such words were regarded with enthusiasm: the mid sixteenth century was also the period at which *inkhorn term* made its appearance. An *inkhorn* was a small portable vessel for ink, and an *inkhorn term* was a word regarded as too bookish or learned. George Puttenham, writing in 1589 in *The Art of Poesie*, identified a number of words (including *irradiation* and *depopulation*) which had been viewed unfavourably, since they were for a long time 'despised for inkhorne termes'.

Towards the present

From the sixteenth century onwards, war, trade, and exploration all brought new words: some coming directly from the language of origin, others passing through intermediate languages. Some Spanish words appearing in English in the sixteenth century reflect the earlier history of the Iberian peninsula and reach back to Arabic roots: for example, *alcalde* (a mayor or magistrate) and *artichoke*. Other words were the fruit of Spanish exploration in the New World: for example *guava* and *iguana*. *Amok* (as in 'run amok'), ultimately from Malay *amuk* 'fighting furiously', came into English in the early sixteenth century via the intermediate Portuguese *am(o)uco*. *Tea* came (probably via Malay) from Chinese. The Middle East contributed such terms as *kaftan* and *yogurt* (from Turkish) and *bazaar* and *turban* (from Persian).

Increasing contact with new and non-European languages impacted on the vocabulary of English. Long involvement with the Indian subcontinent added *bungalow*, *kedgeree*, and *rupee* from Hindi, among a host of other terms. Words and phrases of Chinese origin added from the eighteenth century onwards include *feng shui*, *kowtow*, and *tofu*. *Tycoon*, from Japanese, was originally the title given by foreigners in the mid nineteenth century to the shogun of Japan. Words from Australian Aboriginal languages recorded from the nineteenth century include *kangaroo* and *kookaburra*; the same period saw the addition of Maori *haka* and *kiwi* from New Zealand, and Afrikaans *trek* from South Africa.

In the nineteenth and twentieth centuries, while borrowing from other languages continued, words were also coined or adapted in English worldwide as new materials and processes required names—something which of course is still happening today. When the first fascicles of the *OED* were published, *plastics* had not been invented: in recent decades dictionaries have had to cope with the swiftly changing vocabulary of the *cyber* age. As soon as *email* or *texting* has been covered, it is likely that a new term (such as *tweet*) will be clamouring for attention.

By the end of the twentieth century, terms like 'World English' and 'Global English' were in use. But, along with the recognition of such language areas as 'American English', 'British English', and 'Indian English' as members of a wider grouping, has come a much greater likelihood that we will encounter each other's forms of English. The development of modern communications, and especially use of the internet, ensure that people throughout the world encounter directly forms of English other than their own. There has never been a more promising time to encounter, and explore, unfamiliar and enticing words.

Overview of Dictionary History

DICTIONARIES as we know them today have (like language) evolved from earlier forms. While an academic study may trace their origins back to glossaries in medieval manuscripts, it is in the seventeenth century that we find the first books that we would recognize as English dictionaries. The key date is 1604, the year of the publication of Robert Cawdrey's *A Table Alphabeticall, conteyning and teaching the true writing and understanding of hard usuall English words, borrowed from the Hebrew, Greek, Latin or French*. These 'hard words', learned adoptions into English, were interpreted by 'plaine English words'; the intention was to make the meanings clear to 'ladies, gentlewomen, or any other unskilfull persons' who might have encountered them 'in Scriptures, sermons, or elsewhere'.

The title page, naturally enough, opens the window on to a world which culturally differs notably from our own, and Cawdrey's dictionary is naturally a very different conception from anything we would expect in an English dictionary today. However, before seeing this simply as a reference book from and for the past, it may be salutary to wonder how often we ourselves use a dictionary to look up 'hard words', and how often we consult it for the 'plain English words' about which we may feel we already know.

The importance of Cawdrey's dictionary is that it was the first monolingual English dictionary. It was followed by other, larger collections: for example Thomas Blount's *Glossographia* of 1656, which went much further in the direction of including the wider language. (A particular interest, as Blount said in his 'Note to the Reader', was the specialized vocabulary of different tradesmen: the cook, the vintner, the haberdasher, the tailor.) Others followed, and some proved to be of some longevity. In 1658, Edward Phillips published *The New World of English Words*. It borrowed heavily from Blount, and occasioned considerable ill-feeling, but it lasted: a revised and augmented edition by John Kersey, the *New World of Words, or, Universal English Dictionary*, was published in 1706, with a third edition in 1721.

The same year saw the appearance of Nathan Bailey's *An Universal Etymological English Dictionary: comprehending the derivations of the generality of words in the English tongue, either ancient or modern*. The *Oxford Dictionary of National Biography*'s entry for Bailey, considering the long-lived popularity of his dictionaries, notes both real and fictional admirers, from the first Earl of Chatham to George Eliot's Adam Bede, who 'had read . . . a great deal of Bailey's dictionary.' Bailey was used by 'the great lexicographer' (as Boswell called him), Samuel Johnson.

Johnson's *A Dictionary of the English Language*, published in 1755, is a landmark. The coverage included the wider vocabulary, and meanings and senses were based on a description of how the language was actually used, in many cases illustrated with 'examples from the best writers'. Nothing like it, or on its scale, had existed before. It set a standard for future dictionaries in its coverage and authority, while recognizing that the language it described would continue to change. (As Johnson wrote in his Preface, 'No dictionary of a living tongue can be perfect, since while it is hastening to publication, some words are budding, and some falling away.')

The following century saw major developments in dictionary publishing, in which further key elements in dictionary-making with which we are familiar today made their appearance. In 1828, across the Atlantic, another famous name entered the world of lexicography. Noah Webster, a schoolmaster from Connecticut, published his *American Dictionary of the English Language*, a comprehensive two-volume dictionary which also recognized the distinctive character of American English. Less literary than Johnson, this dictionary's focus was on the up-to-date language, with senses ordered according to current primary meaning rather than chronology, and illustrative quotations restricted to instances where exemplification was required.

Webster himself died in 1840, but further editions were published by the Merriam brothers (who had bought the rights from his heirs). The description 'Webster's unabridged', indicating the completeness of coverage offered, was in use from the mid nineteenth century. Finally, in 1890, came a greatly expanded version of the dictionary, with an alteration of title indicating its breadth of coverage (including special attention paid to scientific and technical vocabulary): *Webster's International Dictionary of the English Language*.

American dictionaries pioneered other features to be found today in dictionaries of current English. One of these was the inclusion of encyclopedic material, a move away from a traditional distinction (which was clearly set out in the Preface to the first edition of the *Concise Oxford Dictionary*):

> The book is designed as a dictionary, and not as an encyclopaedia; that is, the uses of words and phrases as such are its subject matter, and it is concerned with giving information about the things for which those words and phrases stand only so far as correct use of the words depends upon knowledge of the things.
> —H. W. and F. G. Fowler (eds) *Concise Oxford Dictionary*, 1911, Preface, p. iii

Large-scale dictionaries of current English today are likely to include such encyclopedic entries as biographies and names of countries, as well as lexical definitions. The text may also be augmented by pictorial illustration, as was notably done in the great American enterprise *The Century Dictionary*, originally issued in parts between 1889 and 1891, which appeared complete in six handsome volumes in 1891. This major encyclopedic dictionary contained not only around five hundred thousand definitions with many thousands of illustrative quotations, but also eight thousand pictorial illustrations. Today pictorial illustration is also a key feature of Houghton Mifflin's *The American Heritage Dictionary*. The fourth edition, published in 2006, has full-colour marginal illustrations throughout the volume.

Historical dictionaries also found their full form in the nineteenth century. 1837 marked the publication in Britain of Charles Richardson's *A New Dictionary of the English Language*. Richardson's particular vision was for a dictionary of the historical language. He identified four key periods in the history of the language between the medieval and the nineteenth centuries, and he attempted to provide, for all the words covered, quotations to illustrate usage in the periods during which the word had been current. This evidence, in his view, was a satisfactory substitute for definitions. The result was a dictionary which might not be ideal for someone who simply wanted to know the meaning of a word or sense in their own day, but which offered a fascinating picture for someone who was interested in the history of that word.

1884, a landmark year, saw the publication of the first part, or fascicle, (A–ANT) of what was then the *New English Dictionary*, to be completed in 1928 as the twelve-volume *Oxford English Dictionary*: the most complete historical record of the language in existence. Senses were of course ordered chronologically, and the evidence on which definitions and senses were based was printed. The illustrative quotations provided did not simply offer examples of how a word or sense *might* be used, they constituted chronological evidence for the usage.

By the end of the nineteenth century, then, two main categories of dictionary had been established. One strand produced what we would now call dictionaries of the current language ('synchronic'): dictionaries whose purpose is to provide definitions and other information about words which are in use in the language today. Definitions open with the primary modern sense.

The other strand ('diachronic') produced the great historical dictionaries, pre-eminent among them the *Oxford English Dictionary* and its *Supplements*, in which the organization of an entry follows a different pattern. The first use is the earliest recorded, and the entry as a whole offers a biography of a word.

Dictionaries of 'the English language' have a vision of the mainstream English language, although in all of them there is likely to be overlap with some specialist areas—for example, dialect or regional terms, or the language of an earlier period. But in due course, prodigies of effort ensured that material for specialist areas was collected, and dictionaries written. Joseph Wright's *English Dialect Dictionary* was published in 1905. The *Scottish National Dictionary*, begun in 1931, was completed in 1975. In the United States, the *Dictionary of American English on historical principles* (1936–44) and the *Dictionary of Americanisms on historical principles* (1951) gave historical accounts of American English. In the second half of the twentieth century other varieties of English such as Australian, Caribbean, Newfoundland, and South African acquired their own historical dictionaries. For those concerned with the medieval language, the *Dictionary of the Older Scottish Tongue* (1937–2002) and the *Middle English Dictionary* (1952–2001) offered rich resources. Finally, the remarkable *Dictionary of American Regional English*, of which the first volume appeared in 1985, is approaching completion.

Today all major dictionaries have an online presence: in no other way could a complex multi-volume dictionary be regularly updated and maintained. Websites are likely to offer ancillary material, such as articles about usage, spoken pronunciations, or links to other relevant data. There are also resources which were born online: for example, *Wiktionary* and *Dictionary.com*. We have come a long way from Robert Cawdrey, but we can still recognize the impulse that would have driven his readers: the need to find out what a word or sense means, and the likelihood that one answer will prompt another question.

Where to Look: a selection of online resources

WHILE (as we have seen) the internet can offer a bewildering range of possible places to search, the following suggests some initial language sites for word enthusiasts to explore.

Dictionaries

Dictionaries are of course the first place to look, with the *Oxford English Dictionary* providing the most detailed account of the historical language. Typically, with reference sources of this kind, we are looking at data which was originally compiled in hard copy, but which has now moved online. Specialist dictionaries cover particular areas of the language, such as period (the *Middle English Dictionary* for medieval English) and region (the *Dictionary of the Scots Language*).

Not all dictionaries, of course, are available online, but a major dictionary or thesaurus published in hard copy may be supported by a website which offers valuable ancillary material: for example, the *Dictionary of American Regional English* and the *Historical Thesaurus of the Oxford English Dictionary*.

Collaborative online resources such as *Wiktionary* may offer a first view of recent coinages which have not yet been included in traditional dictionaries.

General dictionaries

Dictionary.com
http://dictionary.reference.com

A site offering a dictionary, a thesaurus, and an encyclopedia. Ancillary material includes a crossword solver, word games, and a weekly 'Word Explorer' podcast on the history of words.

TheFreeDictionary

http://www.thefreedictionary.com/dictionary.htm

A free site providing access to the text of the fourth edition (2006) of Houghton Mifflin's *American Heritage Dictionary*, augmented with the second edition of Collins *Essential English Dictionary*. The site includes a thesaurus and an encyclopedia.

Oxford Dictionaries Online

www.oxforddictionaries.com

Launched in 2010, and providing fully searchable content from Oxford's largest modern English dictionaries and thesauruses. Regularly updated to reflect current meanings and new words. Background information includes extensive grammar and spelling guidance, and specialist language reference resources for writers and editors, as well as a puzzle solver section for language lovers and word enthusiasts.

Oxford English Dictionary

www.oed.com

The basis of *OED* online is the Second Edition of 1989, which itself conflated the original *Oxford English Dictionary* (1884–1928) with the four modern *Supplements*, published between 1972 and 1986. The *OED* is currently undergoing a full revision, with quarterly updates in which a particular alphabetic range is revised and updated; the release also includes new words and revised entries from across the alphabet. A full list of words covered is provided, and there is editorial commentary on the batch as a whole.

Searching can cover the whole text, or be limited to specific areas (for example, etymologies or definitions). Background material includes a History of the Dictionary.

Wiktionary

http://en.wiktionary.org

A collaborative dictionary set up as a lexical companion to *Wikipedia*. Ancillary material includes a thesaurus and a rhyme list.

Specialist dictionaries

Australian National Dictionary

http://203.166.81.53/and

The text of *The Australian National Dictionary: A Dictionary of Australianisms on Historical Principles*, originally published in 1988 by the Australian Dictionary Centre, a joint initiative of the Australian National University and Oxford University Press, and now available online. No whole-text searching, but readers can select and call up individual entries in full.

Dictionary of American Regional English

http://dare.wisc.edu

The *Dictionary of American Regional English* (1985–) is approaching completion, with four volumes already published, and the fifth and final volume announced for 2010. The *DARE* website is a rich resource for information about the project and its speciality. As well as an account of the original fieldwork (supported by personal accounts in the Newsletter, which goes back to 1991), there is an index which allows the reader to look up which entries have a particular etymology (for example, words thought to come from Gaelic), or are associated with a particular area (for example, Georgia).

Dictionary of the Scots Language

http://www.dsl.ac.uk

The *Dictionary of the Scots Language* comprises electronic editions of two major dictionaries. The twelve-volume *Dictionary of the Older Scottish Tongue* (*DOST*), covering the language between the twelfth and the seventeenth centuries, was published between 1937 and 2002. The ten-volume *Scottish National Dictionary* (*SND*), which covered the language in use since the beginning of the eighteenth century, appeared between 1931 and 1975. The DSL site makes it possible to search both texts. Additional material includes maps and a history of Scots to 1700.

Middle English Dictionary
http://quod.lib.umich.edu/m/med
The twenty-eight volume *Middle English Dictionary*, compiled between 1952 and 2001, is now available as an electronic resource with full-text searching. The website provides full information as to ways of searching (for example, looking for words and phrases in the text of illustrative quotations, or searching by date). Helpful background support includes suggestions on how to navigate the question of spelling, given that the spelling of a word may vary according to date, place, and even the individual preference of a particular scribe.

Urban Dictionary
http://www.urbandictionary.com
An online site for slang words and phrases, founded in 1999. Entries and definitions are submitted by contributors: according to the home page: 'Urban Dictionary is the dictionary you wrote. Define your world.' Given the speciality of the site, entries are noticeably less sedate than those of dictionaries and sites which focus on more traditional areas of language.

Thesauruses

As indicated above, many dictionary sites include a thesaurus as part of their essential functionality.

Historical Thesaurus of the Oxford English Dictionary
http://libra.englang.arts.gla.ac.uk/WebThesHTML/homepage.html

This major project, published in two volumes in 2009, has analysed the *Oxford English Dictionary* and allotted all words and senses to categories of shared meaning, from a broad category like 'War' to a more specific one, such as a kind of weapon. It is thus possible to find all the words which over the centuries have been used to mean *knife* or *dagger*. To use this resource as a whole, it is necessary to consult the print volumes, but the *Historical Thesaurus of English* website has very helpful information, and does make a number of sections available online.

Visual Thesaurus
http://www.visualthesaurus.com
An interactive dictionary and thesaurus, whose scope includes historical figures, trademarks, and phrases.

Corpora

The development of the language corpus, in which very large sets of data can be searched for words and phrases in context, has ensured that dictionaries can increasingly be based on real-life language use.

British National Corpus (BNC)
http://www.natcorp.ox.ac.uk/corpus
A one-hundred-million word collection of samples of the written and spoken language from a range of sources, representing a wide cross-section of British English from the later part of the twentieth century.

Corpus of Contemporary American English (COCA)
http://www.americancorpus.org
A four-hundred-million word collection of the spoken and written language, representing a wide cross-section of American English from 1990.

Time *Magazine Corpus*
http://corpus.byu.edu/time
A one-hundred-million word corpus of American English, representing the written language in *Time* Magazine from 1923 to the present day.

Word sites

Interest in language has led to the development of a number of sites where all aspects of vocabulary are commented on and analysed. Each site has its own identity (some are the brainchild of an individual enthusiast), but as a group they are united by a fascination with words, and an ability to register and reflect on language change.

Word.com: The Merriam-Webster Online Newsletter
http://www.word.com
A monthly publication by Merriam-Webster which includes notes on the most-looked-up word for that month, and a Word History of the month, plus comments on other words in the news. There is also a report from *Merriam-Webster's Open Dictionary*, where readers are invited to submit entries for new words that they have come across.

WordNet
http://wordnet.princeton.edu
A lexical database of the English language, which groups words into sets of synonyms as well as providing short general definitions.

Wordnik
http://www.wordnik.com
Launched in 2009, a relative newcomer which offers example sentences of real language use to show a word in context, to back up definitions from several dictionaries, as well as a list of synonyms.

Word Spy: the Word Lover's Guide to New Words
http://www.wordspy.com

Paul McFedries's site, launched in 1995, posts definitions of new words and phrases, such as *libel tourist* and *cyberdisinhibition*, supported by illustrative quotations to show usage.

World Wide Words

http://www.worldwidewords.org

Michael Quinion's site on word origins and word histories, which covers both established words which have come to his attention, and new words and phrases which may not yet have appeared in any dictionary. The site includes a *Dictionary of Affixes*, based on Quinion's *Ologies and Isms: Word Beginnings and Word Endings* (2002).

Other

Sites for language projects (complete or ongoing) often provide a wealth of information on particular aspects of the language.

Australian Voices

http://clas.mq.edu.au/australian-voices

This site for Macquarie University's project on languages in Australia includes information on the history and character of Australian English, supported by audio illustrations.

Sounds Familiar

http://www.bl.uk/learning/langlit/sounds

A British Library site providing information about regional vocabulary and pronunciation in the United Kingdom.

Voices

http://www.bbc.co.uk/voices

Site for the BBC project, running between 2005 and 2007, aimed at recording and evaluating regional variations of the spoken word across the United Kingdom. The site includes voice recordings and a word map.

Key Tips for Searching

- **Be aware of what is available.**

Which main reference resources are now available online? What kinds of search do they make possible? What other resources are there? What ancillary material do special websites have?

- **Know your sources.**

Understand what particular reference works offer. Does a particular dictionary focus on the current or the historical language? Does it specialize in a region/period/mode of speech?

- **What special access might you have?**

Do you have a route to resources that are otherwise restricted? For example, readers in Britain are likely to have access to *OED*, the *Times* Digital Archive, and other subscription services through their public library website.

- **Formulate the question clearly: what exactly do you want to know?**

When searching for information about a word, what exactly is it that you want to know? Framing the question to focus on meaning/ origin/usage is likely to point you towards a particular resource.

- **What clues does the word give you?**

Does the look of it suggest a certain language of origin? Does it seem to belong to a particular subject area? Does it belong to a particular set?

- **What clues does the context give you?**

Is there a suggestion that it goes back to a particular year or century? Is it associated with anyone famous? Is the usage from the past (for example, it occurs in a historical novel)?

- **What strategies have worked before?**

Have you done other successful searches which might suggest the best route for this one?

- **Lateral thinking: what connections can you make?**

Systematic searching has come to a dead end: can you 'think sideways', and make a guess at where else you might look?

- **Know when to stop.**

Recognize that, despite your best efforts, only luck will take you further.

Glossary

archaic indicating that a word comes from an earlier period and is no longer in everyday use.

citation a quotation from a book, newspaper, or other source, taken for the purpose of illustrating use of a particular word.

coinage the invention of a new word (a *neologism*).

combining form the form of a word which is used in combination with another element to form a word, as *Anglo-* 'English' in *Anglo-Irish*, and *bio-* 'life' in *biology*.

corpus a collection of written and spoken material, in machine-readable form, assembled for linguistic research.

derivation the formation of a word from another word, or from the root of another word.

derivative a word which is derived directly from another word or from the root of another word, often by the addition of a *suffix*.

descriptive applied to dictionaries which are compiled with the primary intention of describing actual language use rather than recommending what is seen as correct (*prescriptive*).

diachronic concerned with the way in which language has developed over time; used to designate the coverage of a dictionary of the historical language (as contrasted with *synchronic*).

dialect a particular form of language which is peculiar to a specific region or social group.

dictionary a book which lists the words of a language in alphabetical order and gives their meaning; traditionally distinguished from an *encyclopedia* in its coverage.

encyclopedia a book, arranged alphabetically, giving information on many subjects or on many aspects of one subject; traditionally distinguished from a *dictionary* in its coverage.

etymology the study of the origin and history of words; *etymology* is used specifically for the section of a dictionary entry which explains the origin of the headword.

false friend a word which has a similar form to one in another language but a different meaning, as English *magazine* and French *magasin* 'shop'.

figurative not having the literal meaning of the words; metaphorical.

ghost word a word which has been included in a dictionary, but which has never had any real-life language use, and which is likely to owe its existence to a misunderstanding or misreading (for example, *knise* for *knife*).

grammatical relating to the system and structure of a language, especially in relation to the arrangement of words and phrases (*syntax*), and the forms of words (*morphology*).

hard words in the sixteenth century, the term coined to designate words derived from classical languages to fill a gap in the English vocabulary; more generally, words regarded as difficult and unusual, as distinct from those staple in the everyday language.

headword   the word with which an entry in a dictionary begins and which is the subject of the entry.

homograph   a word which is spelled in exactly the same way as another, but which may be pronounced differently, and which has a different meaning and origin (as the *bow* of a ship, and ribbon tied in a *bow*).

homonym   a word which has the same spelling or pronunciation as another, but a different meaning and origin (as *pole*, a long slender piece of wood, and *pole*, a location on the earth's surface).

homophone   a word which is pronounced exactly the same as another, but which has a different meaning, origin, or spelling (as *new* and *knew*).

inflection   the change in the form of a word (typically the ending) which indicates a change in grammatical status, as from present to past tense of a verb, or singular to plural case of a noun.

label   a descriptive word in a dictionary entry which specifies the subject area, register, or geographical origin of a word or sense.

lemma   a word or phrase defined in a dictionary or entered in a word list; the *lemmas* within a dictionary comprise the set of headwords together with all compounds, derivatives, and other items which appear as part of an entry and do not have separate entry status of their own.

lexicographer   a writer or compiler of dictionaries.

lexicon   the complete vocabulary of a person, language, or branch of knowledge.

literal	taking words in their most basic sense, with no metaphorical interpretation.
metaphorical	of the application of a word or phrase to a word or object to which it is not literally applicable (*metaphor*).
morphological	relating to the forms of words, in particular inflected forms (*morphology*).
neologism	a newly invented word or expression.
obsolete	of a word or phrase which was current in an earlier period but which is now no longer used at all.
orthographical	relating to the conventional spelling system of a language (its *orthography*).
prefix	an element added to the beginning of a word to alter or qualify its meaning, as *ex-*, *non-*, *re-*.
prescriptive	applied to dictionaries which have a primary purpose of recommending correct usage, rather than simply describing actual language use (*descriptive*).
register	a particular level of language usage determined by degree of formality and choice of vocabulary, pronunciation, and syntax, which in a dictionary may be indicated by a particular label (as *archaic*, *dialect*, *slang*).
root	in terms of word formation, a meaningful unit which cannot be divided into further parts, and from which words are made by adding prefixes or suffixes or by other alteration.
semantic	relating to meaning in language.
stem	the root or main part of a word, to which inflections or formative elements such as prefixes and suffixes are added.

suffix an element added to the ending of a word to form a derivative, as *–ation*, which forms nouns denoting an action or the instance of an action (as *exploration, hesitation*), or the result or product of an action (as *plantation*).

synchronic concerned with a language as it exists at one point in time; used to designate the coverage of a dictionary of the current language (as contrasted with *diachronic*).

syntactic relating to the arrangement of words and phrases to create well-formed sentences in a language (its *syntax*).

thesaurus a book that lists words in groups of synonyms and related concepts.

transferred of the sense of a word or phrase which has been changed by extension to cover more than the original literal meaning.

unabridged of a text, not cut or shortened; in American lexicography, used to designate a dictionary which represents the most comprehensive coverage of its kind.

Endnotes

Chapter 1

1 It is already found in a number of online sites, such as *Wikipedia* and the *Urban Dictionary* (www.urbandictionary.com).

2 *Webster's New International Dictionary of the English Language*, first published as a single volume in 1909. *Funk and Wagnall's New Standard Dictionary of the English Language*, first published in 1913. *The New Century Dictionary*, first published (initially in three volumes, later in two) in 1927.

3 Rosamund Moon 'Objective or Objectionable? Ideological Aspects of Dictionaries' in *English Language Research Journal* vol. 3, 1989, p. 63.

4 Quoted in Peter Kemp (ed.) *The Oxford Dictionary of Literary Quotations* (2nd edn, 2003).

5 This is likely to affect the way in which information appears, especially in sense ordering. A historical dictionary will give the earliest senses of a word first; a dictionary of current English will give the main current senses first.

6 For a full discussion of major dictionaries, see Chapter 5.

7 Which at the time of writing, March 2010, seems likely.

8 Further useful discussion of how words originate, as well as details of specific examples, is to be found in Susie Dent's series of books *The Language Report*, published in five separate volumes between 2003 and 2007.

9 While it is possible that an overlap of usage evidence may mean that a vocabulary item of this kind could be found in the *Oxford English Dictionary* (it does have an entry for the verb *gar*), a specialist dictionary where one exists is likely to be much more satisfactory.

10 For a more detailed account of this resource, see 'Overview of Dictionary History', p. 157.

11 *Oxford Thesaurus of English* (3rd edn, 2009).

12 A usage which probably comes from Milton's *Paradise Lost*, 'The parching air burns frore.'

13 For more details, including a history of the project, see the *Oxford English Dictionary* website at http://www.oup.com/online/ht.

14 Currently in its 10th edn, published 2009.

Chapter 2

1 Ira Gershwin 'Let's Call the Whole Thing Off', song, 1936.

2 See p. 49.

3 For more on key languages which have contributed to English, see 'Pathways of English', p. 147.

4 See page 25.

5 See further, chapter 6, p. 92.

6 Notably, in the *Oxford English Dictionary*, currently in the process of revision. However, much of the *OED* still represents the unrevised entries first published between 1884 and 1928. It is therefore well worth being aware of the burgeoning possibilities of finding antedatings to the dates given, by searching the online sources made available by the digitization of historical newspapers and other texts.

7 A dictionary entry may well indicate a particular restriction by the use of a label, such as *dialect* or *archaic*, on the headword as a whole or on a specific sense.

Chapter 3

1 For example, *adder*, in which the original initial *n-* of the word was understood as being part of the preceding article in 'an adder', and *apron*, which followed the same pattern.

2 The fascicle covering this term, PLAT–PREMIOUS, was published in 1907; the inclusion indicated that even though there was no illustrative quotation given, *Portugal onion* was regarded as a term which had some familiarity, and which should therefore be in the dictionary.

3 *Skinny* also applied to fashionably tight-fitting clothes dates from the first part of the twentieth century.

4 *Oxford Dictionary of English* (2nd edn revised, 2005).

5 *Merriam-Webster's Collegiate Dictionary* (11th edn, 2003).

6 *Collins English Dictionary* (9th edn, 2007).

7 The process is illuminatingly described in Jeremy Butterfield's book on the topic *Damp Squid: the English language laid bare* (2008).

8 The compound *whippet-thin* gets over fifty hits for the same period; *supermodel-thin* occurs five times.

Chapter 4

1 See also 'Where to Look: a selection of online resources', p. 163.
2 See p. 166.
3 *Oxford Dictionary of English* (2nd edn revised, 2005).
4 *Collins English Dictionary* (9th edn, 2007).
5 *Merriam-Webster's Collegiate Dictionary* (11th edn, 2003).
6 For a discussion of electronic sources, see p. 163.
7 See the *Oxford Dictionary of National Biography*'s entry for the remarkable Joseph Wright, who began life as an illiterate mill-boy.
8 See further, p. 68.
9 There is, for example, reassurance that American English is not being 'homogenized', although the language is changing, and former regional boundaries for linguistic use may be shifting.
10 Once a CD-ROM has been created, it can of course be upgraded to a new version with increased functionality.
11 See p. 15.

Chapter 5

1 Another phrase of some longevity; one regrettable example comes from a review in the *New Monthly Magazine* of April 1831, in which a reviewer of Samuel Lover's *Legends and Stories of Ireland* told their readers: 'We shall offer one word of advice as to the mode of becoming acquainted with its contents—namely, to skip over the "Introduction".'
2 A French word, from Spanish *santo* 'saint'.
3 It is tempting to add 'Provence' to the list, but while this dramatically reduces the number to five, the *Atlantic Monthly* hit does not come up.
4 Regrettably, the article did not provide any specific examples, but the emphasis seems to have been on pronunciation.
5 The original comment was apparently made (in Yiddish) by an unidentified student in 1944, after a lecture given by Weinreich. For full details, see the entry for Max Weinreich (1893–1969) [*sic*] in Fred R. Shapiro *The Yale Book of Quotations* (2006).
6 *Lobscouse*, from which *Scouse* itself comes, is recorded from the early eighteenth century, but its origin is unknown.

Chapter 6

1 For a detailed and fascinating account of the story, see Herbert C. Morton *The Story of Webster's Third* (1995).

2 As in Michael Quinion's *Port Out, Starboard Home: and other Language Myths* (2004).

3 Noël Coward 'I Went to a Marvellous Party' (song, 1936), quoted in *Oxford English Dictionary*, see *gay* adj., sense 4d.

4 The *Oxford Dictionary of Proverbs* (5th edn, 2009), which includes the saying 'A lie is halfway round the world before the truth has got its boots on' (recorded in this form from the mid nineteenth century), points out that the speed with which falsehood travels was a commonplace in the classical world; Shakespeare's evocation of Rumour ultimately looks back to Virgil.

Chapter 7

1 'Blue Moon' was the title of a 1934 popular song by Richard Rodgers and Lorenz Hart, which over the years was recorded by numerous musicians and singers including Louis Armstrong, Ella Fitzgerald, Elvis Presley, Billie Holliday, and Bob Dylan.

2 See *Oxford English Dictionary* entry for *moon* n.[1], under phrase *to believe that the moon is made of green cheese*.

Chapter 8

1 Jeanette Winterson *Oranges are not the Only Fruit* (novel, 1983).

2 While this sense (also *Satsuma pottery* or *Satsuma ware*) still exists in English, it is clear from dictionaries of current English that *satsuma* as a fruit is now the primary sense of the word.

3 Exploration via Google Books reveals that General Van Valkenburg had been American Minister to Japan (Albert Bigelow Paine *Mark Twain, a biography* (1935)).

4 A number of websites carry the information, presented without cavil, that the fruit was developed in 1832 by a Philip Satsuma of Osaka. He is said to have grafted a branch from a tangerine tree on to a mandarin orange, using cuttings from a kumquat. This sounds extremely precise, but attempts to get back to the source of the information have failed, and no specific references are given. It seems likely that this is an instance of an internet-circulated etymology which needs to be regarded with considerable scepticism, if not outright disbelief.

5 For a further discussion of this word, see p. 133.

6 A useful way to look at an *OED* entry for this information is to use the 'Date chart' button, which provides a layout including a dateline for each sense.

7 The full reference for the diary in question supports the Japanese origin of the fruit; it was published in 1883 under the title *Diary in Japan 1615–22*. Richard Cocks, the author, has an entry in the *Oxford Dictionary of National Biography*, where he is described as 'merchant and East India company servant'.

8 This of course gives us another name for the list, and in turn offers further possibilities for exploration. The name *pomelo* (recorded in English from the early nineteenth century) may be an alteration of the earlier (late seventeenth century) *pampelmoes* (an early kind of *grapefruit*), which now survives mainly in South African English. It is also called the *shaddock*, a name which was first recorded in the late seventeenth century, and apparently comes from the name of an East-India Captain who introduced the fruit into the West Indies in the seventeenth century. According to Sir Hans Sloane's *A Voyage to the Islands Madera, Barbados, Nieves, S. Christophers, and Jamaica, with the Natural History of the last* (1707–25), as quoted in the *OED* entry for *shaddock*, 'The seed of this was first brought to Barbados by one Captain Shaddock, Commander of an East-India Ship, who touch'd at that Island in his Passage to England, and left the Seed there.'

9 The importance of its colour as a characteristic of the fruit might prompt the question, what other of the names on our list have themselves become names for a shade between red and yellow? A quick search of *OED* definitions for 'orange colour' leads us to *tangerine*, but not to other names. It would however be possible to extend the search to other online sources for terms which would not produce an impossible number of results. The site *LitFinder* searched in this way supplies a reference, from Oliver Marshall's poem 'The King's Shilling' in Angela Greene and Oliver Marshal *Trio Poetry 6* (1990), to 'Clonmel's deep red and satsuma-tinted sky'.

10 If using Google Books, limitation of publication date to the last few years, and view to 'Limited preview', should ensure that the number of hits is not overwhelming (and might have the benefit of offering access to a modern edition of an older text), and will allow you to see enough of the context to be useful.

11 In one well-known reference, the citrus fruit in question is a lemon. In 1918, at the end of the First World War, the British politician and administrator Eric Geddes promised that 'The Germans, if this Government is returned, are going to pay every penny; they are going to be squeezed as a lemon is squeezed—until the pips squeak' (speech at Cambridge, 10 December 1918, quoted in the *Oxford Dictionary of Quotations* (7th edn, 2009)).

12 Quoted in *OED*.

13 1822 in *G. Canning and his Times*; this source is available in full text on Google Books, and consultation of it reveals that the letter was written to a personal friend a few weeks after Canning had become Foreign Secretary.

14 *Sex and Sensibility* (1986); quoted in *OED*.

15 Ernest Gruening *The State of Alaska* (1968), p. 21 (Google Books); original source is said to have been the *New York World*, 1 April 1867.

16 *Oxford Dictionary of National Biography* (online edition), 'Nell Gwyn'.

17 P. G. Wodehouse *Right Ho, Jeeves* (1934).

Subject index

Word index

•••